MW00612484

Understanding
IRS Communications

Third Edition

CCH Editorial Staff Publication

CCH INCORPORATED
Chicago

A WoltersKluwer Company

ISBN 0-8080-1236-3

Preface

Thorough tax research, planning, advice, and return preparation are predicated on a basic understanding of IRS documents and communication. This understanding is critical for litigation and dealings with the IRS as well.

Understanding IRS Communications provides you with a working description of key IRS documents. It also discusses their legal effect and importance for tax planning and research. It serves tax practitioners, government employees, educators, and students as a useful reference, textbook, or training aid.

Increased Availability and Variety of IRS Documents. Congress has mandated that the IRS publicly disclose an increasing volume of IRS documents including internal IRS communications, as well as communications which were formerly privately provided to taxpayers. The Taxpayer Bill of Rights required the IRS to disclose certain rights of taxpayers and explain procedures in nontechnical terms. The Electronic Freedom of Information Act Amendments of 1996 mandated that governmental agency records be made available electronically, and, thus, numerous IRS documents are now available on the Internet.

In enacting Internal Revenue Code Sec. 6103—Confidentiality and Disclosure of Returns and Return Information, Code Sec. 6110—Public Inspection of Written Determinations, and Code Sec. 7805—Rules and Regulations, Congress redefined the scope for publication and disclosure of IRS documents. Numerous court decisions have addressed the requirement to disclose and the precedential value of such documents.

What to Rely on and When. *Understanding IRS Communications* identifies and describes, in plain rather than highly technical language, the myriad of IRS documents. The degree of reliance on such documents and the retroactive application of new or modified IRS positions are discussed where pertinent (in .05 and .10, respectively, of each paragraph). Summaries of the reliance and retroactivity rules appear at ¶111 and ¶112.

Appendices—Sample Documents. Appendices include sample key documents, a chart on the precedential value of IRS documents, guidelines for determining the effect of revenue rulings and revenue procedures on previous rulings, and a listing of commonly referenced documents, with abbreviations.

October 2004

Table of Contents

Chapter 1

Introduction

¶1 IRS Communications—90 Years in the Making

More than 90 years ago, the Sixteenth Amendment to the United States Constitution (¶12), which granted power to Congress to levy and collect taxes on incomes without apportionment among the states, was adopted. Since passage of the first income tax laws, the Internal Revenue Service (IRS) has engaged in major publication efforts to provide taxpayers and their advisors with the most current interpretative views of all areas of federal income tax law.

¶2 Publication Efforts

From its meager issuance of the first income tax regulations in 1914 consisting of 170 pages[1] to the plethora of documents published today, the IRS has become a major distributor of information impacting the tax lives of all Americans.

Demands for advance information interpreting federal tax laws have increased as tax planning has emerged as a major industry impacting economic growth and stability in the United States. Numerous major tax packages have been enacted in the last two decades. The Tax Reform Act of 1986, being the most complex and comprehensive modification in history, spawned more than 2,700 revisions. Publication of advance information has become an essential element in the federal tax system as a tool for assuring uniform taxpayer compliance.

The degree of reliance that taxpayers may afford advance information depends on the authority of the legal sources giving rise to the pronouncement.

A paper entitled "The Four R's: Regulations, Rulings, Reliance, and Retroactivity—A View from Within" was presented by Mitchell Rogovin, former Chief Counsel of the Internal Revenue Service, at the 18th Annual Tax Conference conducted at the University of Chicago Law School.[2] Although Mr. Rogovin's paper was not an "official" release and, thus, does not necessarily represent the views of the Treasury Department or the Internal Revenue Service, it continues to be informative and revealing in the manner in which it analyzes the communications issued by the Internal Revenue Service, their degree of reliability, and the Commissioner's power to retroactively change or modify the position taken in the different types of communications.

Since that paper, there have been major changes in document disclosure laws promulgated by Congress, as well as changes resulting from actions of the IRS and by court decisions.

---

[1] Treas. Reg. 33 (1914).

[2] Mitchell Rogovin, "The Four R's: Regulations, Rulings, Reliance and Retroactivity: A View from Within," 43 *TAXES—The Tax Magazine* 756.

¶4 IRS Positions—Tracing the Legal Sources

In a society governed by laws, the degree of reliance that may be afforded a government pronouncement depends on the authority of the legal sources giving rise to the pronouncement. It is important, therefore, in determining the degree of reliance to be placed on IRS positions to consider the ultimate legal authorities underlying those pronouncements.

Since the United States is a constitutional government, fundamental authority is, of course, derived from the Constitution (¶11). The Constitution provides for three separate (but in many cases overlapping) branches of legal authority: Legislative (¶20-26), Executive (¶30-38), and Judicial (¶40-46). The legal authority of each of the three branches of government directly influences the content and scope of IRS organizational structure (briefly described herein) and IRS positions.

The branches of government

A basic discussion of the inner-workings of the three branches of government is essential in tracing the roots of authority and reliance on various IRS pronouncements. In a sense, every IRS position can be viewed as consisting of a legislative, judicial, and executive component.

The development, interpretation, and administration of internal revenue laws by these exclusive but interacting branches of government has resulted in taxpayers' demands for timely advance information and guidance to assure, to the greatest degree possible, uniform compliance and fair tax administration. Disclosed IRS positions and information disseminated by private publishers provide invaluable input for the overall tax system.

Legislative: In the case of Legislative Branch authority, the reliance issue is clear since Congress creates the statutes that establish legal requirements. Therefore, any IRS position that fails to accurately interpret a statute has no legal effect and is unenforceable (¶71). The IRS strives to glean legislative intent in formulating official positions. How well the IRS expresses legislative intent impacts the ultimate degree of reliability (¶46).

Judicial: Similarly, the role of the judiciary in questions of reliance is basic— what a court determines on a particular IRS position is final as to the parties involved (subject to appeals) and has great weight in establishing legal principles on which taxpayers can reasonably rely. Once again, the IRS strives to formulate positions that give great deference to prevailing legal opinions as expressed by the courts. The degree of reliance that may be reasonably placed on IRS positions depends on the success of the IRS in incorporating the prevailing legal opinions.

The role of the judiciary, however, is not without limitations. For example, the IRS may disagree with the legal reasoning of the Tax Court in a particular case and, at its option, issue a nonacquiescence (¶42). A nonacquiescence puts taxpayers on notice that reliance on the Tax Court's decision would be risky and that such reliance would likely be resolved only by future litigation with the IRS.

Executive: Unless an issue has been settled by a decision of the Supreme Court (¶45), the IRS (i.e., the Executive Branch) can, in effect, ignore the Tax Court's legal reasoning in formulating positions. If an issue has been settled by Supreme Court decision, that decision is binding on taxpayers and the IRS and, thus, the IRS must incorporate the Supreme Court's legal reasoning into official IRS positions until and unless the Legislative Branch modifies the law. Executive Branch enforcement and interpretation considerations also include the revenue impact, the cost of litigation, and other administrative policies, goals, and constraints.

¶5 Disclosure Laws

Disclosure laws impact on the availability of IRS positions and background documents detailing the formulation of rules and procedures for interpretation, implementation, and administration of federal tax laws. The Freedom of Information Act (¶61), the Tax Reform Act of 1976 (¶62), and the Privacy Act (¶63) were instrumental in the development of disclosure rules that affect all taxpayers. Congress passed a Taxpayer Bill of Rights (¶64), which gives taxpayers certain rights in dealing with the IRS and includes expanded disclosure provisions. More recently, the Electronic Freedom of Information Act Amendments of 1996 and the IRS Restructuring and Reform Act of 1998 required the IRS to provide electronic access to many documents (¶67).

Exemptions available for denying access to documents, or limiting disclosure to those individual taxpayers directly involved in an investigation or audit are enumerated (¶65). Individuals also are affected by "practical reliance" on decisions by IRS personnel at all levels in the administrative process even when documentation of such decisions is not publicly disclosed.

¶6 Practical Reliance and Nondisclosure

Exemptions from disclosure (¶65) result in nondisclosure of documents that are prepared during the course of an investigation. Taxpayers who do not challenge decisions of IRS personnel having an impact on their individual returns, through the appeals process, if available, or through the courts, are considered to concede the accuracy of such interpretations. This "practical reliance" on IRS positions arguably affects the individual returns and any future returns of a great percentage of taxpayers who might be affected by such interpretations.

Five-prong test for analyzing authority

One cannot analyze authority in a vacuum. Thus, the following five-prong analysis[3] is necessary:

1. *WHY is the determination of authority relevant to the tax practitioner?* Is the advice being given to provide a tax return preparer with comfort in taking a questionable reporting position on a tax return? Is the client

---

[3] Sheldon I. Banoff, "Dealing with the 'Authorities': Determining the Valid Legal Authority In Advising Clients, Rendering Opinions, Preparing Tax Returns and Avoiding Penalties," 66 *TAXES—The Tax Magazine* 1072, 1074 (December, 1988).

willing to be aggressive as to his tax liability but highly concerned about avoiding penalties? Is advice being given to a client as to whether his position will stand up if challenged in court?

2. *WHAT is the universe of authorities?* What are the potential types of legal authority that one might identify, e.g., the Internal Revenue Code, regulations, cases and various IRS pronouncements?

3. *WHICH of the authorities (in item 2) count for purposes of the practitioner's relevant concern (in item 1)?* It is critical to determine whether the potential authority upon which the practitioner wishes to rely is valid authority for purposes of the operative issue. As illustrated herein, many types of authority are recognized for some purposes but not for others.

4. *HOW are the valid, relevant authorities (in item 3) weighed for purposes of the practitioner's relevant concern (in item 1)?* Assuming there are authorities in the practitioner's favor, how much weight do they carry? If there are also authorities against the practitioner, what is their weight? If the authorities are conflicting, how should they be weighed?

5. *WHAT standard of authority must the practitioner meet, for purposes of his operative concern?* For example, does he merely need sufficient authority to support a "reasonable basis" for success? Does he need "substantial authority"? Does he require more favorable than unfavorable authority, so he can issue a "more likely than not" legal opinion?

¶7 IRS Positions

A definition and discussion of key positions taken by the IRS and communicated through a myriad of publications and disclosures are provided. Particular emphasis is placed on the degree of reliance and retroactive application of such documents.

Key documents include:

Regulations and Treasury Decisions (¶71-¶73);

Revenue Rulings (¶74);

Revenue Procedures (¶75);

Private Letter Rulings (¶81);

Technical Advice Memoranda (¶83);

General Counsel Memoranda (¶92);

Actions on Decisions (¶93);

Pre-filing Agreements (¶89);

Chief Counsel Advice (¶96);

Field Service Advice (¶97);

Taxpayer Assistance Orders (¶106);

Industry Specialization Program Papers (¶93) and

Market Segment Specialization Program Papers (¶95).

Internal Revenue Manual (¶76);

Commissioner Delegation Orders (¶77);

Chief Counsel Orders and Notices (¶78);

Determination Letters (¶82);

Opinion Letters (¶84);

Information Letters (¶85);

Technical Memoranda (¶86);

Outgoing Treasury Letters (¶87);

Closing Agreements (¶88);

Pre-filing Agreements (¶89);

Technical expedited advice (¶90);

LMSB Directives (¶98);

Technical Information Releases and News Releases (¶103);

Pamphlets and Handbooks (¶104);

IRS Publications (¶101);

Forms and Instructions (¶102);

Announcements (¶79);

Notices (¶79); and

Acquiescences (¶42).

Publication requirements and the evolution of disclosure laws have revolutionized the availability of documents.

Key IRS documents that are voluntarily disclosed to the public or are discoverable under court rules are addressed. No attempt is made to discuss each document that might be produced during the IRS tax preparation, submission, review, audit, and appeals process. Thus, for example, documents prepared during the course of an audit or investigation, such as audit reports and collection action reports, are not discussed.

¶8 Special Features

Special aids are provided to facilitate research. First, sample key documents (¶120) illustrate specific examples and structure of documents published and disclosed by the IRS. Sample documents include: notice of proposed rulemaking; regulation; Treasury decision; revenue ruling; revenue procedure; private letter ruling; announcement; notice; action on decision; chief counsel advice; field service advice; litigation guideline memo; market segment specialization guide; industry specialization program paper; Internal Revenue news release; and other key communications.

Several other special aids contribute to a basic understanding of IRS positions:

Precedential Value of IRS Documents (¶121): A chart listing key IRS documents and indicating the precedential value of each.

Keywords Used to Explain New or Revised Rulings (¶122): A listing of terms that describe the effect of new or revised revenue rulings and revenue procedures on previous rulings.

Research Documents and Source Materials (¶123): An alphabetical listing of IRS documents and source materials that are commonly used for tax research. (Some of the documents and source materials are included for completeness only. Discussion of such documents and source materials is not contained herein.)

Abbreviations for Research Documents and Source Materials (¶123): An alphabetical listing of commonly used abbreviations in IRS documents and source materials (¶123).

CCH Incorporated Publications (¶124): A partial listing of CCH Incorporated publications that routinely publish, summarize, and explain Internal Revenue Service publications.

Chapter 2
The Federal Tax System

¶10 Overview

To better understand the policies and procedures that have evolved for interpretation, promulgation, disclosure, publication, and reliance on IRS positions, it is essential to focus on the underlying legal authority. The degree of reliance that may be placed on IRS positions depends on diligent adherence to powers so granted.

Fundamental to any discussion of the federal tax system is a review of key provisions of the United States Constitution (¶11). Authority derived from the Constitution and the need to adapt to a changing society led to the adoption of the Sixteenth Amendment (¶12), which provided for a tax on income from "whatever source derived"—the cornerstone of modern-day income tax law. The first income tax act (¶13), which enumerated the authority derived from the Sixteenth Amendment, was the initial legislative act authorizing a general tax on income. Since that time, numerous tax acts have been passed by Congress within the framework of the separation of powers doctrine (¶14) delineated in the Constitution.

¶11 Constitution

General taxing powers were granted to the Congress by the United States Constitution that stated:

> The Congress shall have power to lay and collect taxes, duties, imposts and excises, to pay the debts and provide for the common defense and general welfare of the United States ....[1]

This federal taxing power was limited by two provisions:

1. "But all duties, imposts, and excises shall be uniform through the United States."[2]

2. "No capitation, or other direct, tax shall be laid, unless in proportion to a census or enumeration herein before directed to be taken."[3]

The second limitation required that any direct tax must be apportioned among the states on the basis of population. The amount to be collected first had to be apportioned, and then the rates had to be fixed separately in each state so as to produce the quota apportioned to it.[4] To free itself from this limitation, the Congress proposed an amendment to the Constitution—the Sixteenth Amendment (¶12).

---

[1] Constitution of the United States, Art. I, Sec. 8.
[2] Constitution of the United States, Art. I, Sec. 8.
[3] Constitution of the United States, Art. I, Sec. 9.
[4] *Hylton v. United States*, 3 Dall. 171 (1796).

¶12 Sixteenth Amendment

The Sixteenth Amendment to the Constitution was adopted on February 25, 1913. It provided that:

> The Congress shall have the power to lay and collect taxes on incomes from whatever source derived, without apportionment among the several States, and without regard to any census or enumeration.

Since the sole purpose of this amendment was to eliminate the requirement of apportionment in the case of taxes on all incomes, its effect was limited.[5] The amendment did not free the taxing power of Congress from any other limitations. Thus, unless the tax could be classified as "income," the power of Congress to impose direct taxes still was limited by the requirement of apportionment.

¶13 First Income Tax

Soon after adoption of the Sixteenth Amendment, on October 3, 1913, Congress enacted the first income tax law. This law was retroactive and provided for a tax on all income arising on or after March 1, 1913, from "whatever source derived." Since 1913, numerous income tax acts have been passed by Congress.

Based on the doctrine of separation of powers, the Legislative, Executive, and Judicial Branches of the federal government have significantly contributed to the continuing development of the federal tax system.

¶14 Separation of Powers

The separation of powers among the branches of the federal government was delineated by the framers of the Constitution as follows:

Article I. Legislative (¶20)

Article II. Executive (¶30)

Article III. Judicial (¶40)

A brief discussion of the separation of powers doctrine is essential to a basic understanding of the respective, intermixed powers of the Legislative, Executive, and Judicial Branches with respect to the development and promulgation of income tax regulations and rulings (¶71 and 74). These dynamic, but separate, branches each have an impact on the degree of reliance on IRS positions, as well as the issue of retroactivity.

---

[5] *Evans v. Gore*, SCt, 1 USTC ¶36, 253 US 245.

¶12

Chapter 3
Legislative Powers and the IRS

¶20 Overview

The Legislative Branch plays an instrumental role in the development and enactment of income tax laws and laws that impact executive and judicial authority. Official IRS positions that implement and interpret the laws are developed within the framework of legislative intent. Legislative acts, unless determined by the courts to be unconstitutional, are binding on taxpayers and the IRS and, thus, are the very essence of reliance.

Legislative authority to create statutes and agencies to enforce the laws derives from the Constitution (¶21). Recognizing the need to codify internal revenue laws to provide conclusive proof of the existence and wording of any provision, Congress enacted the Internal Revenue Code (IRC) (¶22). To implement the IRC, the Legislative Branch designated the Treasury Department (¶23) to supervise administration and enforcement of the federal tax laws and created the Internal Revenue Service (¶24) to collect the tax revenues. The Legislative Branch maintains an active role in the internal revenue laws process partially through the Joint Committee on Taxation (¶26). This congressional oversight directly influences tax administration and enforcement policies.

Administrative Procedure Act

Recognizing the need to address the procedural formalities to which federal agencies, including the IRS, must adhere during the decision-making process, Congress adopted the Administrative Procedure Act (APA) (¶25). The APA established rules for publication, disclosure, and dissemination of IRS positions and other pronouncements. Although these procedures are now relatively routine, they are still essential in determining the degree of reliance that may be placed on IRS positions.

¶21 Constitutional Powers

The United States Constitution provides that Congress shall have the power to "make all Laws which shall be necessary and proper" for execution of its enumerated powers.[1] Most of the tax statutes enacted by Congress appear officially under the title of "Revenue Act." Originally, the various Revenue Acts were published in the "Statutes at Large," a series of volumes that contained all the federal statutes as passed. In 1924, the United States Code was prepared as an official restatement of the general and permanent laws of the United States. The Code incorporated the internal revenue laws as Title 26.

---

[1] Constitution of the United States, Art. I, Sec. 8.

¶22 Internal Revenue Code

Because the Code was only presumptive evidence of the law and because conclusive proof of the existence and wording of any provision still required reference to the Statutes at Large, Congress codified Title 26 and reenacted the Internal Revenue Code, thus making it conclusive evidence. This codification was accomplished on February 10, 1939, and entitled the "Internal Revenue Code" (IRC). To be all inclusive, the IRC repealed and reenacted all the internal revenue laws then in force.

Fifteen years later, Congress again codified all the income, estate, gift, and excise tax laws, along with administration and procedure rules, into an instrument called "The Internal Revenue Code of 1954." Revision of the Internal Revenue Code by the Tax Reform Act of 1986 was so extensive that it was renamed "The Internal Revenue Code of 1986."

¶23 Treasury Department

The Constitution provides that "Congress may by Law vest the Appointment of such inferior Officers, as they think proper, in the President . . . or in the Heads of Departments."[2] Congress has put the administration of federal taxation into the hands of the Department of Treasury, one of the oldest departments of the Executive Branch of the federal government.

On July 1, 1862, the Office of the Commissioner of the Internal Revenue was established by an act of Congress. The Act provided that, "for the purpose of superintending the collection of internal duties, stamp duties, licenses, or taxes imposed by this Act, or which may be hereafter imposed, and of assessing the same, an office is hereby created in the Treasury Department to be called the Office of the Commissioner of the Internal Revenue."[3]

Congress has provided that administration and enforcement of the Internal Revenue Code, except as otherwise provided by law, be performed by or under the supervision of the Secretary of the Treasury.[4] The Treasury Secretary (¶32), General Counsel (¶33), IRS Commissioner (¶34), and Assistant General Counsel—Chief Counsel of the IRS (¶35) are appointed by the President with the advice and consent of the Senate.[5]

¶24 Internal Revenue Service

The IRS has existed since 1913, when the adoption of the Sixteenth Amendment (¶12) authorized Congress to "lay and collect taxes on incomes from whatever source derived . . . ." The task of collecting the internal revenues was entrusted to the Internal Revenue Service. Although the title was never formally adopted, for many years this agency was known as the Bureau of Internal Revenue. On July 9, 1953, the Treasury Department ordered that henceforth it was to be designated as the Internal Revenue Service.[6]

---

[2] Constitution of the United States, Art. II, Sec. 2.
[3] 12 Stat. 432.
[4] Code Sec. 7801(a).

[5] Code Secs. 7801(b) and 7803(a).
[6] T.D. 6038, 1953-2 CB 443.

The functions of the operating divisions are to be undertaken in light of the IRS's new mission statement, to "provide America's taxpayers top quality service by helping them understand and meet their tax responsibilities and by applying the tax law with integrity and fairness to all." This mission statement was mandated by the IRS Restructuring and Reform Act of 1998. The legislation required the IRS "to review and restate its mission to place a greater emphasis on serving the public and meeting taxpayers' needs."[7]

IRS Strategic Goals:

(1) provide top-qualify service to each taxpayer in every interaction;

(2) provide top-quality service to all taxpayers through fair and uniform application of the law; and

(3) increase productivity within the IRS by providing IRS employees with a quality work environment.

After enactment of the IRS Restructuring and Reform Act of 1998, the IRS began to reorganize certain activities into Operating Divisions.[8] This structure resulted in individual taxpayers being classified in either the **Wage & Investment Operating Division** (W&I) or in the **Small Business/Self Employed** (SB/SE) Operating Division.[9] Most compliance operations for W&I are performed by correspondence through the various Service Centers, also called Campuses. SB/SE compliance functions are located in field offices arranged into Areas headed by Area Directors (AD) and further divided into Territories and headed by Territory Managers (TM).

Territory Managers oversee the activities of Group Managers who supervise the first line employees such as Tax Compliance Officers (TCOs) and Revenue Agents (RAs).

The **Large and Mid-Sized Business** (LMSB) operating division has jurisdiction over C corporations, S corporations, and partnerships with assets equal to or greater than $10 million.

The **Tax-Exempt and Government Entities Division** serves the needs of three customer segments: Employee Plans, Exempt Organizations, and Government Entities. Customers range from small local community organizations and municipalities to major universities, huge pension funds, state governments, Indian tribal governments, and complex tax-exempt bond deals. The Tax-Exempt and Government Entities Division has approximately 2,400 employees and serves approximately 3 million entities.

As the chief legal advisor to the IRS Commissioner on all matters pertaining to the interpretation, administration, and enforcement of the Internal Revenue Laws, as well as all other legal matters, the **Chief Counsel** provides legal guidance and interpretive advice to the IRS, Treasury, and to taxpayers.

---

[7] Act Sec. 1002 of the IRS Restructuring and Reform Act of 1998 (P.L. 105-206).

[8] IRS Pub. 3349 at 33-40.

[9] IRS Pub. 3349 at 34; IRS 1

The **Taxpayer Advocate Service** helps taxpayers resolve problems with the IRS and recommends changes to prevent the problems.

Criminal Investigation looks for potential criminal violations of the Internal Revenue Code and related financial crimes in a manner that fosters confidence in the tax system and compliance with the law.

The **Appeals** function serves as the administrative forum for any taxpayer contesting an IRS compliance action.

Communications & Liaison supports the IRS mission and business objectives using strategic relationship management, communication tools and processes, resolution of issues of mutual concern, and information sharing.

The chief executive officer of the IRS is the IRS Commissioner (¶34). The Commissioner is also the principal spokesperson for the IRS with Congress.[10]

¶25 Administrative Procedure Act

In 1946, recognizing the need to address the procedural formalities to which federal agencies, including the IRS, must adhere during the decision-making process, Congress adopted the Administrative Procedure Act (APA). Like the Internal Revenue Code, the APA has now been codified and also is conclusive evidence of the law.[11] The major purposes of the APA were: (1) to introduce greater uniformity of procedure and standardization of administrative practice among diverse agencies the customs of which departed widely from each other and (2) to curtail and change practices embodying in one person or agency the duties of prosecutor and judge.[12] The APA includes the following:

1. definitions establishing the Act's terms and coverage;
2. requirements for publication of certain rules and regulations in the *Federal Register* (¶51);
3. requirements for federal agencies to make other important decisions and documents available for public inspection and copying (¶66); and
4. procedural formalities that agencies must observe during the decision-making process (¶70).

¶26 Congressional Oversight

Congress maintains its role in the internal revenue laws process partially through the Joint Committee on Taxation, composed of ten members selected from two congressional committees. Five members are selected from the Senate Committee on Finance and five from the House of Representatives Committee on Ways and Means.[13]

---

[10] Code Sec. 7803.
[11] 5 U.S.C. § 551, *et seq.*

[12] *Wong Yang Sung v. McGrath,* 339 US 33, modified on other grounds, 339 US 908.
[13] Code Secs. 8001 and 8002.

Powers

The Joint Committee on Taxation has the power to:

1. Obtain data and inspect income tax returns;
2. Hold hearings;
3. Require by subpoena or otherwise the attendance of witnesses and the production of documents;
4. Administer oaths;
5. Take testimony; and
6. Procure printing and binding.[14]

Duties

The Joint Committee's 10 members have the duty to:

1. Investigate the operation and effects of the federal system of internal revenue taxes;
2. Investigate the administration of taxes by the IRS or any executive department or agency;
3. Make other investigations relative to the tax system;
4. Investigate measures and methods for the simplification of taxes;
5. Publish proposed measures and methods for the simplification of taxes; and
6. Report to the Committees on Finance and Ways and Means and, in their discretion, to the Senate or House of Representatives the results of their investigations.[15] The IRS Restructuring and Reform Act of 1998 (P.L. 105-206) requires the Joint Committee on Taxation to review all requests by the GAO for investigations of the IRS. Certain requests originating from the chair or other ranking member of a House or Senate committee or subcommittee are excepted from this requirement.[16] The Joint Committee on Taxation is also required to make regular reports to Congress on the overall state of the federal tax system.[17]

---

[14] Code Sec. 8021.
[15] Code Sec. 8022.

[16] Code Sec. 8021(e).
[17] Code Sec. 8022(3).

Chapter 4
Executive Authority and the IRS

¶30 Overview

The Executive Branch is authorized by the Constitution (¶31) to execute the laws enacted by the legislative branch. Internal revenue laws are administered and enforced through promulgation of IRS positions. Responsibility for development, approval, dissemination, and implementation of IRS positions is established by legal authority.

The Internal Revenue Code (¶22) provides for the appointment by the President of the United States of a Treasury Secretary (¶32), IRS Oversight Board (¶37), General Counsel—Treasury (¶33), IRS Commissioner (¶35 who administers the IRS National Office ¶34), Treasury Inspector General for Tax Administration (¶37) and Assistant General Counsel—Chief Counsel of the IRS (¶36) to administer and enforce the tax laws and to collect tax revenues. The National Taxpayer Advocate (¶39) was established by Congress in 1998 to provide assistance to taxpayers who have problems with the IRS.

The Executive Branch, unless limited by law, has authority to develop appropriate organizational structures and procedures to carry out its missions. Enumerated powers and duties of these officials assist in development of an overall understanding of the system for publication, disclosure, and dissemination of IRS positions and other pronouncements. This organizational structure has a direct bearing on reliance issues.

¶31 Constitutional Powers

It is the duty of the President of the United States to "take Care that the Laws be faithfully executed . . . ."[1] The President also has the power to "nominate, and by and with the Advice and Consent of the Senate, . . . appoint . . . Officers of the United States . . . which shall be established by Law . . . ."[2]

The law specifically authorizes the President to appoint, with the advice and consent of the Senate, the Treasury Secretary (¶32), General Counsel for the Department of the Treasury (¶33), IRS Commissioner (¶34), and Assistant General Counsel—Chief Counsel of the IRS (¶36).[3]

¶32 Treasury Secretary

The administration and enforcement of federal internal revenue laws must be performed by or under the supervision of the Secretary of the Treasury.[4] Except where such authority is expressly given to any officer or employee of the Treasury Department, the Treasury Secretary is authorized to prescribe and

---

[1] Constitution of the United States, Art. II, Sec. 3.
[2] Constitution of the United States, Art. II, Sec. 2.
[3] Code Secs. 7801(b) and 7802(a).
[4] Code Sec. 7801(a).

publish all rules and regulations (¶70) necessary for enforcement of internal revenue laws.[5]

The power to invest the Treasury Secretary with authority to prescribe regulations has been held to be constitutional, so long as such regulations are not inconsistent with the law.[6] However, "arbitrary" regulations are not authorized[7] and, if devoid of any rational basis, regulations may be determined by the court to be an abuse of discretion.[8] In addition, construction of a statute by the IRS, the department charged with bringing it into effect, is given great weight by the courts (¶71).[9]

¶33 General Counsel—Treasury

The General Counsel for the Department of the Treasury also is appointed by the President with the advice and consent of the Senate. The General Counsel functions as the chief law officer of the Treasury Department and is responsible for such duties as may be prescribed by the Treasury Secretary.[10] The President also has authority to appoint, with the advice and consent of the Senate, an Assistant General Counsel who functions as the Chief Counsel for the IRS.[11]

¶34 IRS Commissioner

Federal tax laws are administered and enforced under the supervision of the Secretary of the Treasury. The Treasury Secretary delegates the responsibility for administering the tax laws to the IRS Commissioner. The IRS Commissioner is the official immediately in charge of the IRS. The IRS Restructuring and Reform Act of 1998 (P.L. 105-206) made specific changes to the Commissioner's duties, qualifications and term of office.

Any IRS Commissioner appointed is required to have, among other qualifications, a "demonstrated ability in management."[12] The IRS Commissioner is appointed to serve a five-year term.[13] The Commissioner remains an appointee of the President, with advice and consent of the Senate, and may be removed at any time by the President.

The duties of the IRS Commissioner, all of which are subject to delegation by the Treasury Secretary, are:

(1) to administer, manage, direct and supervise the execution and application of the tax laws and tax treaty provisions; and

(2) to recommend candidates for Chief Counsel to the President when a vacancy occurs and recommend the removal of Chief Counsel.

---

[5] Code Sec. 7805(a).

[6] *Brushaber v. U.P. Railroad Co.*, SCt, 1 USTC ¶4, 240 US 1.

[7] *J. Weidenhoff, Inc.*, 32 TC 1222, CCH Dec. 23,761 (Acq.).

[8] Code Sec. 7805(b); *W.K. Baker*, CA-11, 85-1 USTC ¶9101, 748 F2d 1465, aff'g DC Ga., 84-1 USTC ¶9110, 575 FSupp 508.

[9] *Burk-Waggoner Oil Ass'n v. Hopkins*, SCt, 1 USTC ¶143, 269 US 110.

[10] Code Sec. 7801(b)(1).

[11] Code Sec. 7801(b)(2).

[12] Code Sec. 7803(a)(1)(A).

[13] Code Sec. 7803(a)(1)(A).

If the Treasury Secretary decides not to delegate any of these powers, all six of the Congressional committees with jurisdiction over the IRS must first be notified (the House Committees on Ways and Means, Government Reform and Oversight, and Appropriations, and the Senate Committees on Finance, Governmental Affairs, and Appropriations).[14]

The IRS Commissioner is required to consult with the Oversight Board on issues relating to operational functions of the IRS, such as plans for modernization, managed competition, or training and education.[15]

¶35 Chief Counsel

The Chief Counsel is appointed by the President with the advice and consent of the Senate.[16] The Chief Counsel's powers are delegated by the Treasury Secretary. These powers are to include the duty to be the legal advisor to the Commissioner and to IRS officers and employees; to furnish legal opinions for the preparation and review of rulings and technical advice memoranda; to prepare, review and assist in preparing proposed legislation, treaties, regulations and executive orders relating to laws affecting the IRS; to represent the Commissioner before the Tax Court; and to determine which civil actions under the Code should be litigated and to recommend to the Justice Department the commencement of such actions.[17]

The offices in the National Office that have jurisdiction over tax subject matter include the Office of the Associate Chief Counsel Passthroughs and Special Industries, Procedure and Administration, Income Tax and Accounting, Corporate, International, and Financial Institutions and Products.

Each office is divided into branches that have jurisdiction over particular code sections or issues (subject matter jurisdiction). More than one branch can have jurisdiction over a particular code section or issue. A Branch Chief oversees each branch. Within each branch, there is generally an Assistant to the Branch Chief and two or more managers called Senior Technician Reviewers. The remainder of the attorneys in the branch are docket attorneys. Generally, a taxpayer and/or a taxpayer's representative will meet with attorneys at the National Office only if the taxpayer has requested a Private Letter Ruling, a Technical Advice Memorandum, a Technical Expedited Advice Memorandum, or is testifying at a regulation hearing.

The Chief Counsel reports directly to the IRS Commissioner except in the following circumstances:

(1) with respect to legal advice or interpretation of tax law not relating solely to tax policy and with respect to tax litigation, the Chief Counsel is to report to both the Commissioner and the General Counsel for the Treasury Department; and

---

[14] Code Sec. 7803(a)(2).
[15] Code Sec. 7803(a)(3).

[16] Code Sec. 7803(b)(1).
[17] Code Sec. 7803(b)(2).

(2) with respect to legal advice or interpretation of tax law relating solely to tax policy, the Chief Counsel is to report to the General Counsel only.[18]

If there is any disagreement between the Commissioner and the General Counsel with any matter that is jointly referred to them, the matter is to be submitted to the Treasury Secretary or Deputy Secretary for resolution.[19]

¶36 IRS Oversight Board

Congress has created a nine-member IRS Oversight Board with actual authority to control actions taken within the IRS. The Board is responsible for overseeing the IRS in its administration, management, conduct, direction and supervision of the execution and application of the internal revenue laws or related statutes and tax treaties.[20]

Specifically, the Board will ensure that the IRS is organized and operated to carry out its mission.[21] In carrying out its duties, the Board is to exercise "appropriate confidentiality."[22]

The nine board members will consist of six individuals who are not otherwise Federal officers or employees, plus the Treasury Secretary (or Deputy Treasury Secretary), the IRS Commissioner, and an individual who is a full-time Federal Employee or a representative of employees (the employee representative). The private-sector members and the employee representative must be appointed by the President with the advice and consent of the Senate.[23]

The Board is to make sure that taxpayers are properly treated by IRS employees.[24] Operational functions at the IRS will be subject to Board scrutiny. The Board is responsible for reviewing IRS plans for modernizing the tax system, outsourcing, managed competition and training and education.[25]

The Board is also specifically required to be involved in strategic planning at the IRS. As part of its strategic planning role, the Board reviews and approves the establishment of IRS strategic plans, including annual plans, long-range plans, and any other missions and objectives related to strategic planning. Performance standards related to any missions and objectives are also subject to review.[26] The Board must review and approve the Commissioner's plans for any reorganization of the IRS.[27]

¶37 Treasury Inspector General for Tax Administration

The Treasury Inspector General for Tax Administration (TIGTA) has the sole authority to conduct an audit or investigation of the IRS Oversight Board and the IRS Chief Counsel;[28] and is responsible for protecting the IRS against external

---

[18] Code Sec. 7803(b)(3).
[19] Code Sec. 7803(b)(3).
[20] Code Sec. 7802(c)(1)(A).
[21] Code Sec. 7802(c)(1)(B).
[22] Code Sec. 7802(c)(1)(C).
[23] Code Sec. 7802(b).

[24] Code Sec. 7802(d)(5).
[25] Code Sec. 7802(d)(2).
[26] Code Sec. 7802(d)(1).
[27] Code Sec. 7802(d)(3)(C).
[28] 5 USC App. §8(d)(h), as added by Act Sec. 1103(b)(7) of P.L. 105-206.

threats to corrupt or threaten employees but is not responsible for conducting background checks and providing physical security.[29]

TIGTA must conduct periodic audits of a statistically valid sample of the total number of denials of written requests to disclose information under the Freedom of Information Act or Code Sec. 6103. Taxpayers must be provided with a toll-free number to confidentially register complaints of IRS employee misconduct.[30]

As an example of a TIGTA report see, "IRS Audit Trail on Computer Systems Not Working," which was issued on September 2, 2004, see *http://www.treas.gov/tigta/*.

¶38 National Taxpayer Advocate

For over 20 years, the IRS has provided some form of assistance to taxpayers who have problems with the agency. The IRS established the Taxpayer Ombudsman Office in 1979. The Office of the Taxpayer Advocate was created by Congress in 1996, replacing the Taxpayer Ombudsman. As a part of the IRS Restructuring and Reform Act of 1998 (P.L. 105-206), the Taxpayer Advocate was renamed the National Taxpayer Advocate. The National Taxpayer Advocate is appointed by the Treasury Secretary, after consulting with the Commissioner and the Oversight Board.[31]

The functions of the National Taxpayer Advocate Office are to:

(1) assist taxpayers in resolving problems with the IRS;

(2) identify areas in which taxpayers have problems in dealing with the IRS;

(3) propose changes to IRS administrative practices that would mitigate the problems identified in item (2) above (to the extent possible); and

(4) identify possible law changes which might mitigate the problems identified.[32]

Each local Advocate's office must maintain means of communication that are independent of the IRS. Each office must have a separate phone, fax machine, and separate post office address, as well as other independent electronic communication access.[33]

When an advocate meets initially with any taxpayer, the advocate must inform the taxpayer that it operates independently of any other IRS offices and that it reports directly to Congress through the National Taxpayer Advocate. The local taxpayer advocate has the discretion not to inform the IRS of any contact with that taxpayer or of any information provided to the local office by the taxpayer.[34]

---

[29] 5 USC App. §8D(k)(1), as added by P.L. 105-206.

[30] Code Sec. 7803(d)(3).

[31] Code Sec. 7803(c)(1)(B).

[32] Code Sec. 7803(c)(2)(A).

[33] Code Sec. 7803(c)(4)(B).

[34] Code Sec. 7803(c)(4)(A).

Deficiency notices must include a notice informing the taxpayer of the taxpayer's right to contact a local office of the Taxpayer Advocate as well as the location and phone number of the appropriate office.[35]

---

[35] Code Sec. 6212(a).

Chapter 5
Judicial Impact on IRS Communications

¶40 Overview

The Judicial Branch is authorized by the Constitution (¶41) to interpret the Internal Revenue Code (¶22) and IRS positions in the context of litigation. Judicial interpretation of the IRC (¶46) may, depending on the circumstances, be based on the language of the statute, Congressional committee reports, reenactment of IRC provisions, or official IRS positions.

Congress created the United States Tax Court (¶42) with limited jurisdiction to adjudicate tax disputes between taxpayers and the IRS. Whenever the IRS loses a Tax Court case, the IRS Commissioner (¶34) has the right, but not the obligation, to formally agree with the decision, called an "acquiescence", or to disagree, called a "nonacquiescence" (¶42).

This procedure has been implemented in an attempt to provide uniformity in the law and to promote fundamental fairness. However, the technique provides the Executive Branch with significant power since the IRS can refuse to recognize the validity of a Tax Court decision and, in effect, force taxpayers to either conform to the IRS view or incur the expense of litigating the issue again.

In addition to the Tax Court, taxpayers have access to U.S. District Courts and to the Court of Federal Claims (¶43). To exercise this right, however, taxpayers must first pay the disputed tax, file a claim for a refund, and have the claim rejected, a time-consuming and expensive process.

Appeals from the Tax Court and other trial courts are directed to a U.S. Court of Appeals (¶44). The opinions of a Court of Appeals carry greater weight of authority than Tax Court opinions. Reviews of decisions of a Court of Appeals are requested by writ of certiorari to the U.S. Supreme Court (¶45). Decisions of the U.S. Supreme Court are final authority as to what a statute means or as to any question of federal law. Since IRS positions cannot be contrary to law, taxpayers and the IRS may, until and unless contrary legislation is enacted, rely on decisions of the U.S. Supreme Court.

¶41 Constitutional Powers

The Constitution provides that "the judicial Power of the United States, shall be vested in one supreme Court, and in such inferior Courts as the Congress may from time to time ordain and establish."[1] The Congress also has the power " . . . to constitute Tribunals inferior to the supreme Court."[2] The United States Tax Court, United States District Courts, United States Court of Federal Claims,

---

[1] Constitution of the United States, Art. III, Sec. 1.

[2] Constitution of the United States, Art. I, Sec. 8, Clause 9.

United States Courts of Appeals, and the Supreme Court review and interpret the IRC and IRS positions in the context of litigation.

¶42 Tax Court

The United States Tax Court (Tax Court)—known prior to the Revenue Act of 1942 (1942 Act) as the United States Board of Tax Appeals—was created in 1924 to replace an appeals committee set up in the IRS. Its jurisdiction prior to the 1942 Act was limited to income, excess profits, and estate and gift taxes. Under the 1942 Act, its jurisdiction expanded to include refunds of certain processing taxes.

The Tax Reform Act of 1969 gave the Tax Court the status of a court under Article I, Section 8, Clause 9 of the Constitution.[3]

Cases decided by the Tax Court upon factual determinations alone and cases involving an issue that is considered settled in the law or is only of limited interest are ordinarily classified as memorandum decisions. This classification is part of an effort to keep what is otherwise clear precedential case law free of needless repetition.

Precedent for the Tax Court is generally found in "regular" opinions and especially in those opinions that have been "reviewed by the court." An opinion will be submitted to the entire court for review when the chief judge determines that the issue presented should be considered by all judges on the court. The government printing office publishes both "regular" and "reviewed by the court" decisions in The United States Tax Court Reports. Citations to these volumes are to the volume and page.

Memorandum opinions are not included in the government series of The United States Tax Court Reports. Memorandum opinions, however, together with regular and reviewed by the court decisions, are reproduced in the CCH TAX COURT REPORTER. Memorandum decisions are additionally published by CCH INCORPORATED in permanent, bound editions and are cited as "TCM."

In addition to the formal identification given each case by the Tax Court, CCH assigns each decision, whether "regular" or "memorandum," a number, "CCH Dec.," as soon as it is released by the Tax Court. A memorandum decision is indicated by the letter "(M)" following the decision number.

Small Tax Case

Taxpayers who file a Tax Court petition have the option of having their case heard under expedited and simplified procedures in certain circumstances if the amount of the deficiency, or claimed overpayment, does not exceed $50,000. Although proceedings are judicial in character, small tax cases are conducted as informally as possible. Neither briefs nor oral arguments are required, although they may be permitted by the Tax Court on its own motion or upon request of either party. Decisions in these cases, however, are neither precedent for future cases nor reviewable upon appeal by either the government or the taxpayer.[4]

---

[3] P.L. 100-647, 102 Stat. 3342.   [4] Code Sec. 7463(b).

Acquiescence in Tax Court decisions

Whenever the IRS loses an issue in a litigated Tax Court case, the Commissioner has the option, but not the obligation, to either agree to follow the position of the case or disagree with the court's decision and decline to follow it. Agreement with the court's decision is called "acquiescence" and disagreement is referred to as "nonacquiescence" (see sample Acquiescences and Nonacquiescences at ¶120; see, also, ¶93, Actions on Decisions).

The IRS does not issue acquiescences and nonacquiescences in other than Tax Court cases because it does not have jurisdiction to do so. All other federal courts fall within the jurisdiction of the Justice Department, which controls the litigation, with the advice and guidance of the IRS. On very rare occasions, the Justice Department will designate an IRS attorney as a Special Assistant to the U.S. Attorney to try cases, but the Justice Department retains control over the litigation process. However, when the IRS loses a litigated tax case in the District Court (¶43), Court of Federal Claims (¶43), or Court of Appeals (¶44), the Chief Counsel's Office (¶35) may prepare an Action on Decision (¶93) setting out the reasons for agreeing or disagreeing with the decision.

Generally, the Commissioner will acquiesce when the IRS intends to follow the Tax Court's decision and, thus, will not appeal the decision to a higher court. When the IRS announces an acquiescence in result only, it merely means that the Commissioner, while disagreeing with the treatment by the court of one or more issues, will not file an appeal in the case.[5]

Although there is nothing in the law that makes it compulsory for the Commissioner to appeal a Tax Court decision, a nonacquiescence may indicate his intention to do so. Regardless, a nonacquiescence puts the officers and agents of the IRS and taxpayers on notice that the matter is not settled. This technique may be used by the IRS to forum shop where, for example, there is precedent detrimental to the IRS's position in the circuit where the adverse decision was entered, but supporting the IRS's position in another circuit. In such case, the IRS has the option of waiting for the issue to be litigated in the favorable forum.

Effect of acquiescences

Generally, a taxpayer may rely on an outstanding acquiescence to be the official position of the IRS on issues involving substantially the same facts and circumstances. Taxpayers who rely on a Tax Court decision where the Commissioner has published a nonacquiescence assume a risk. The IRS will likely decide the issue adversely to such taxpayers, and, thus, they too would have to pursue the matter in the courts.

While IRS acquiescence in a case may indicate that one would be likely to obtain a favorable ruling on a similar point, the acquiescence program is not intended as a substitute for the ruling or regulation program (¶71 and ¶74). For example, an outstanding acquiescence in a case involving claim of right advance

---

[5] Rev. Rul. 55-600, 1955-2 CB 576.

rental income did not bar the IRS from collecting tax in contravention of the rule stated in a prior case to which there had been an acquiescence.[6]

Withdrawal of acquiescences

The IRS Commissioner has the right to withdraw an acquiescence and substitute a nonacquiescence. However, this right is not without limitations. For example, it is inequitable for the Commissioner to allow one taxpayer to rely on an acquiescence, but deny reliance to another.[7] On the other hand, the Commissioner is not prohibited from withdrawing an acquiescence where other taxpayers are treated similarly and the taxpayer relying on the acquiescence fails to prove discrimination.[8]

¶43 Other Trial Courts

Other federal trial courts, in addition to the Tax Court (¶42), include U.S. District Courts and the Court of Federal Claims. Access to these trial courts and to the Tax Court differ. To sue in the Tax Court, the taxpayer need not first pay the deficiency in tax asserted by the IRS (but interest will be assessed on the deficiency if the taxpayer loses). However, to sue in a district court or the Court of Federal Claims, the taxpayer must first pay the tax asserted to be due, file a claim for refund of that tax, have the claim rejected by the IRS, and then file suit.

¶44 Courts of Appeals

Appeals from the Tax Court (¶42), and in most cases from a federal district court, are sent to one of 11 U.S. Court of Appeals circuits or to the U.S. Court of Appeals for the District of Columbia. Effective October 1, 1982, Congress created the U.S. Court of Appeals for the Federal Circuit to assume jurisdiction over the appellate functions previously within the purview of the U.S. Court of Claims (now the Court of Federal Claims).[9] Greater weight is given to federal appellate court opinions than those of the Tax Court, U.S. District Courts, and the Court of Federal Claims.

¶45 Supreme Court

To request review of decisions of a Court of Appeals (¶44) the taxpayer must file a petition for a writ of certiorari. The U.S. Supreme Court, however, will in most cases review a decision only where there is a conflict between decisions of the courts below, where the decision is probably in conflict with some prior decision of the Court, or where the issue is considered of major importance. If the U.S. Supreme Court declines to review the decision, the petition for certiorari will be denied. The U.S. Supreme Court is the final authority as to what a statute means or as to any question of federal law.

---

[6] *Quinn*, CA-7, 75-2 USTC ¶9764, 524 F2d 617.

[7] *City Loan and Savings Co.*, CA-6, 61-1 USTC ¶9273, 287 F2d 612.

[8] *Schwartz*, 40 TC 191, CCH Dec. 26,093.

[9] 96 Stat. 25, Federal Courts Improvement Act of 1982.

¶46 Judicial Interpretation of the Internal Revenue Code

Generally, when confronted with the interpretation of the Internal Revenue Code, a court's first duty is to read it in its ordinary and natural sense. If this approach fails to yield satisfactory results, the court will resort to legislative history and prior law.[10] However, recourse may be had to legislative history of an act of Congress where the words are ambiguous or would bring about an end completely at variance with the purpose of the statute if generally construed.[11]

Congressional committee reports

Congressional committee reports, although perhaps providing considerable insight into the underlying intent of a new or revised income tax law, do not govern where the language of the law is determined to be contrary.[12] Although debates in Congress are not a safe guide, reports of committees of the Senate or House of Representatives may be regarded as an exposition of the legislative intent in a case where the meaning of a statute is otherwise obscure.[13]

Reenactment of Code provisions

Generally, reenactment without change of the statute amounts to an implied recognition and approval of the prior IRS construction of the statute.[14] Thus, legislative history, prior laws, committee reports, debates, and construction of language by the courts provide, at a minimum, information essential to understanding and applying income tax laws to specific transactions and circumstances.

---

[10] *H.A. Brody Corp.*, DC Iowa, 61-2 USTC ¶9691, 197 FSupp 918.

[11] *F.H. Gilbert*, CA-9, 57-1 USTC ¶9427, 241 F2d 491.

[12] *Flex-O-Glass, Inc.*, DC Ill., 59-1 USTC ¶9328.

[13] *Hampton & Langley Field Ry. Co. v. Noel*, DC, 300 F. 438.

[14] *Provost v. U.S.*, SCt, 1 USTC ¶153, 269 U.S. 443; *U.S. v. Falk & Bro.*, 204 US 143; *U.S. v. Hermanos*, 209 US 337; *National Lead Co. v. U.S.*, 252 US 140.

Chapter 6

Publication of IRS Positions

¶50 Overview

Publication of IRS positions, advance rulings, determinations, and other pronouncements and information has contributed significantly to a uniform, fair federal tax system. The availability of information has intensified the debate as to the degree of reliance that taxpayers may place on published rulings. The Administrative Procedure Act (APA) (¶25) requires publication of certain rules and regulations, as well as other information, in the *Federal Register*. In many cases, a general notice of proposed rulemaking (NPRM) (¶51) also must be published, and failure to do so directly affects reliance on such pronouncements.

The authoritative instrument of the IRS for publication of official rulings and procedures is the Internal Revenue Bulletin (I.R.B.) (¶52). To preserve a permanent reference source, the contents of the weekly Internal Revenue Bulletin are consolidated semi-annually into an indexed Cumulative Bulletin (CB) (¶53).

¶51 Federal Register

The Administrative Procedure Act (¶25) established requirements for publication of certain rules and regulations in the *Federal Register*.[1] Each agency, including the IRS, must make the following information available to the public by current publication in the *Federal Register*:[2]

1. Descriptions of its central and field organization and the established places at which the employees, from whom, and the methods whereby, the public may obtain information, make submittals or requests, or obtain decisions;

2. Statements of the general course and method by which its functions are channeled and determined, including the nature and requirements of all formal and informal procedures;

3. Rules of procedure, descriptions of forms available or the places at which forms may be obtained, and instructions as to the scope and contents of all papers, reports, or examinations;

4. Substantive rules of general applicability adopted as authorized by law, and statements of general policy or interpretations of general applicability formulated and adopted by the agency; and

5. Each amendment, revision, or repeal of the foregoing.

---

[1] 5 U.S.C. §552.   [2] 5 U.S.C. §552(a)(1).

Notice of proposed rulemaking

A general notice of proposed rulemaking (NPRM) (see sample at ¶120) must be published in the *Federal Register* and must include the following:[3]

1. A statement of the time, place, and nature of public rulemaking proceedings;

2. Reference to the legal authority under which the rule is proposed; and

3. Either the terms or substance of the proposed rule or a description of the subjects and issues involved.

Except when notice or hearing is required by statute, a general notice of proposed rulemaking does not apply to interpretative rules, general statements of policy, or rules of agency organization, procedure, or practice.[4] Also, such notice is not required when the agency, for good cause, finds that notice and public procedure thereon are impracticable, unnecessary, or contrary to the public interest.

The agency issuing a general notice of proposed rulemaking must give interested persons an opportunity to participate in the rulemaking through submission of written data, views, or arguments with or without opportunity for oral presentation.[5] Publication of a substantive rule must occur not less than 30 days before its effective date, except as follows:[6]

1. When a substantive rule grants or recognizes an exemption or relieves a restriction;

2. When the rule published is an interpretation of rules and statements of policy; or

3. As otherwise provided, when an agency finds good cause to publish a rule.

¶52 Internal Revenue Bulletin

The Internal Revenue Bulletin (I.R.B.) is the authoritative instrument of the IRS for publication of official rulings and procedures, including all rulings and statements of procedure that supersede, revoke, modify, amend, or affect any previously published ruling or procedure.[7] Treasury Decisions (¶71), Executive Orders (¶95), tax conventions, legislation, court decisions, announcements of acquiescences and nonacquiescences in decisions of the Tax Court (¶42), and other items considered to be of general interest are also published.

The purpose of publishing revenue rulings (¶74) and revenue procedures (¶75) in the Internal Revenue Bulletin is to promote correct and uniform application of the tax laws by IRS employees and to assist taxpayers in attaining maximum voluntary compliance by informing IRS personnel and the public of IRS interpretations of the Internal Revenue Code, related statutes, treaties, regu-

---

[3] 5 U.S.C. §553(b).
[4] 5 U.S.C. §553(b).
[5] 5 U.S.C. §553(c).

[6] 5 U.S.C. §553(d).
[7] Rev. Proc. 89-14, 1989-1 CB 814; Reg. §601.601(d)(2)(ii).

lations, and statements of IRS procedures affecting the rights and duties of taxpayers.[8]

The Internal Revenue Bulletin is divided into four parts as follows:

Part I. 1986 Code. Part I includes rulings and decisions based on provisions of the Internal Revenue Code.

Part II. Treaties and Tax Legislation. Part II has two subparts: Subpart A, Tax Conventions, and Subpart B, Legislation and Related Committee Reports.

Part III. Administrative, Procedural, and Miscellaneous. To the extent practicable, pertinent cross references to administrative, procedural, and miscellaneous matters are contained in the other Parts and Subparts.

Part IV. Items of General Interest. Part IV includes notices of proposed rulemaking, disbarment and suspension lists, and announcements.

The first Internal Revenue Bulletin for each month includes an index for the matters published during the preceding month. These monthly indexes are cumulated on a quarterly and semiannual basis, and are published in the first Internal Revenue Bulletin of the succeeding quarterly and semiannual period, respectively.

Exceptions to publication requirements

Exceptions to the publication requirements stated above include:

1. Issues answered by statute, treaty, or regulation;
2. Issues answered by rulings, opinions, or court decisions previously published in the Internal Revenue Bulletin;
3. Issues that are of insufficient importance or interest to warrant publication;
4. Determinations of fact rather than interpretations of law;
5. Informers and informers' rewards; or
6. Disclosures of secret formulas, processes, business practices, and similar information.

All published rulings apply retroactively unless otherwise indicated.

¶53 Cumulative Bulletin

In order to provide a permanent reference source, the contents of the weekly Internal Revenue Bulletin (¶52) are consolidated semiannually into an indexed Cumulative Bulletin (CB).

From 1919-1922, there were five volumes of the Cumulative Bulletin, numbered 1 to 5, containing only income tax rulings. There were also three volumes containing only sales tax rulings. The entire series of the Cumulative Bulletin from 1919 to the present, together with the organized bodies of regulations,

---

[8] Rev. Proc. 89-14, 1989-1 CB 814; Reg. §601.601(d)(2)(iii).

comprises a complete source of the official administrative interpretations of the Internal Revenue Code (¶22).

Beginning in 1998, the Cumulative Bulletin is composed of reprints of the weekly Internal Revenue Bulletins issued during the year. Public laws relating to taxes are published in a separate volume. For years prior to 1998, the Cumulative Bulletin presented the I.R.B. documents in three parts: Part I included rulings and decisions arranged according to the Code and regulation sections to which they related; Part II included treaties and tax legislation; and Part III provided items related to administrative, procedural and miscellaneous topics.

Each semiannual Cumulative Bulletin contains an index entry for each item under one of the following titles: employment tax; estate and gift tax administrative; estate tax; excise taxes; and income tax. Each index entry is followed by an abbreviation and number referring to the specific item, i.e., revenue ruling (¶74), revenue procedure (¶75), notice of proposed rulemaking, Treasury Decision (¶71), court decision (¶42), public law, executive order (¶95), delegation order (¶77), Treasury Department order (¶98), tax convention, or Statement of Procedural Rules (¶71).

Chapter 7
Disclosure of Information

¶60 Overview

Legislation that led to the disclosure of advance rulings, determinations, and, with restrictions, intra-and inter-agency memoranda has had a tremendous impact on the federal tax system. As more and more information has become available, controversy has erupted with respect to the appropriate degree of reliance on such documents. The availability of these documents has resulted in reliance on the information contained therein, formally or informally.

The first major legislation having an impact on disclosure of information by federal agencies was the Freedom of Information Act (FOIA) (¶61). The scope of items subject to disclosure was expanded by the Tax Reform Act of 1976 (¶62), which included a provision for disclosure of "written determinations." The Tax Reform Act of 1976 also provided for "sanitizing" documents of all identifying and confidential information before disclosure to conform with requirements of the Privacy Act (¶63). The Privacy Act prohibits unauthorized disclosure by government agencies of information about individuals contained in agencies' systems of record unless such information falls within one of the enumerated exceptions.

The Technical and Miscellaneous Revenue Act of 1988 enacted a Taxpayer Bill of Rights (¶64) that gives taxpayers certain rights in dealing with the IRS. Disclosure of these rights to taxpayers is mandated. These provisions were amended in 1996 by the Taxpayer Bill of Rights 2.

Certain enumerated types of information may not be required to be disclosed, or if required to be disclosed, portions may have to be redacted. Disclosure requirements have been widened by Congress in the IRS Restructuring and Reform Act of 1998 and the Tax Relief Extension Act of 1999 (¶65). Other important decisions and documents must be made available for public inspection and copying (¶66). The Electronic Freedom of Information Act Amendments of 1996 mandated electronic publication of many documents (¶67).

¶61 Freedom of Information Act

In 1967, Congress enacted the Freedom of Information Act (FOIA) as the legal basis for the public availability of federal agency records.[1] However, it was not until 1974 that the law began affecting the disclosure of advance rulings and determinations (¶80) issued by the IRS. At that time, an amendment to the law provided for federal district court review of disclosure requests.

---

[1] *Freedom of Information Act*, 5 U.S.C. §552, Subchapter II.

The IRS had taken the position that unpublished rulings were exempt from disclosure under the FOIA because they were, in effect, tax returns and tax return information.[2] However, the courts disagreed with respect to private letter rulings (¶81) and other written determinations (¶82-88), finding such documents to be subject to disclosure.[3]

Classification of information

The FOIA classifies government information into three categories, with different requirements as to the degree of publicity required.[4]

1. *Information that must be published in the Federal Register* (¶51). With regards to the IRS, this includes regulations (¶71), revenue rulings (¶74), and revenue procedures (¶75);

2. *Information that is not required to be published in the Federal Register, but must be made available for public inspection and copying* (¶66). This includes statements of policy and interpretations that have been adopted by the IRS, as well as administrative staff manuals and instructions to staff that affect a member of the public; and

3. *Documents that a member of the public may obtain by making a request for the information.* Potentially, this includes all information in the hands of the Executive Branch, including the IRS, that is subject to procedures for making such requests, unless the material requested falls into one of the exemptions listed in the FOIA (¶65).

Disclosure requirements under the FOIA have been litigated within the framework of the specified exemptions (¶65). In response to FOIA litigation, after weighing all of the concerns—individual, judicial, and governmental—Congress enacted legislation expanding disclosure to IRS private letter rulings (¶81) and other written determinations (¶82-88).

¶62 Disclosure of Written Determinations

All IRS written determinations, including private letter rulings (¶81), determination letters (¶82), and technical advice memoranda (¶83), prepared pursuant to taxpayer requests are generally open to public inspection, once all identifying details and various commercial and financial information have been deleted.[5] The IRS Restructuring and Reform Act of 1998 added Chief Counsel Advice (¶96), including field service advice (¶97), to the category of written determinations.[6] Special disclosure rules apply to IRS determinations regarding

---

[2] Code Secs. 6103 and 7213.

[3] *Tax Analysts and Advocates*, CA DC, 74-2 USTC ¶9635, 505 F2d 350, modifying and remanding DC Colo., 73-2 USTC ¶9481, 362 FSupp 1298; *Fruehauf Corp.*, SCt, 77-1 USTC ¶9234, 429 US 1085, vacating and remanding, CA-6, 75-2 USTC ¶9554, 552 F2d 284.

[4] John L. Snyder, "Developments on Freedom of Information Act Reveal Trend Toward Greater Disclosure," 50 *The Journal of Taxation* 48, January 1979.

[5] Code Sec. 6110. The effect of adding this provision negated the authority of the FOIA (¶61) as the primary means of disclosure of requests, *Grenier*, DC Md., 78-1 USTC ¶9390, 449 FSupp 834.

[6] Code Sec. 6110(b)(1).

applications for tax exemption of charitable organizations, pension, profit sharing and stock bonus plans, and individual retirement accounts and annuities.[7]

The Tax Relief Extension Act of 1999 excluded advance pricing agreements (APA) from the definition of written determinations.[8] An APA entered into by the taxpayer and the IRS is treated as confidential return information. The IRS is required to publish an annual report providing general information regarding APA filings and executions during the year.[9]

Background file documents

A background file document relating to any written determination of the IRS is also available under the disclosure rules. Such a document includes:

(1) the request for the written determination;

(2) any written material submitted in support of the request for the IRS ruling; and

(3) any communication, received before issuance of written advice, between the IRS and persons outside the IRS as to the written determination.[10]

The Code indicates that the communication in (2) may be "written or otherwise." Presumably, this language is intended to include notes taken by IRS personnel in regard to a telephone or other conversation. The communication in (2), however, does not include a communication, related to a specific determination, between the IRS and the Department of Justice concerning a particular pending criminal or civil case or investigation.

The background file does not include IRS internal memoranda on the IRS's legal position with respect to a particular written determination or the question involved in it.

Requests for background documents concerning letter rulings and technical advice memoranda must be in writing and must include the file number of the documents requested. The request must also specify whether it is for all of the documents in the file or only for a specific item. The various fees assessed for searching, making appropriate deletions, and copying are payable in advance. The requested documents will ordinarily be received between 90 and 120 days after receipt of the document request. A form request example is provided in Rev. Proc. 95-15.[11]

This revenue procedure applies to requests for background file documents (documents) pertaining to a ruling letter or a technical advice memorandum issued by the National Office, but does not apply to a determination letter. The text of any determination letter that is open to public inspection is located in the Reading Room of the Regional Office in which is located the district office that issued the determination letter. Inspection of any background file document can be requested only from the reading room in which the related written determina-

---

[7] Code Sec. 6104.

[8] Code Sec. 6110(b)(1).

[9] Sec. 521(b) of P.L. 106-270.

[10] Code Sec. 6110(b)(2).

[11] 1995-1 CB 523.

tion is either open to public inspection or subject to inspection upon written request.[12]

Tax returns

The IRS probably has more information about more people than any other agency in the United States, thus any federal or state agency needing information about U.S. citizens tends to seek it from the IRS. To protect taxpayers, tax returns and return information are confidential and are not subject to disclosure to federal or state agencies or employees except as specifically provided.[13] Effective July 22, 1998, a plain language explanation of the return confidentiality rules must be included in any instruction booklets sent out to accompany individual income tax forms. The disclosure statement must include a concise statement of the situations in which the information reported on the tax form can be disclosed to a party outside of the IRS (including disclosure to a state, agency, body, commission, or legal representative of a commission).[14] For example, the Taxpayer Relief Act of 1997 permits the disclosure of return information for non-tax administration purposes to certain government agencies including, the Department of Veterans Affairs and the Treasury Department's Financial Management Service.[15]

A full discussion of confidentiality and disclosure of tax returns and return information issues is beyond the scope of this publication.

Third party tax returns

Congress has indicated that it wanted to limit the circumstances under which third-party returns or return information could be disclosed.[16] Statutorily such disclosure is permitted:

(a) if the treatment of an item reflected on such return is directly related to the resolution of an issue in the proceeding, the "item test" (*e.g.* the return of a partnership may reflect the treatment of certain items which may be relevant to the resolution of a partner's liability) or;

(b) if the return or return information directly relates to a transactional relationship between a person who is a party to the proceeding and the taxpayer which directly affects the resolution of an issue in the proceeding, the "transaction test" (e.g. where a third party's return may relate to a transaction between the third party and the taxpayer).[17]

Despite these exceptions case law has narrowly construed Code Sec. 6103(h)(4).[18] However, recently courts[19] have allowed inspection of returns and

---

[12] Reg. § 301.6110-1(c).

[13] Code Sec. 6103.

[14] Act Sec. 3508 of the IRS Restructuring and Reform Act of 1998 (P.L. 105-206).

[15] Code Secs. 6103(l)(7)(D)(viii) and 6103(k)(8).

[16] S. Rep. No. 94-938, 94th Cong., 2d Sess.(1976), at 325-26.

[17] Code Sec. 6103(h)(4).

[18] See, for example, *J. LeBaron*, 92-1 USTC ¶50,089, 794 F. Supp. 947; *M.A. Tavery*, 94-2 USTC ¶50,390, 32 F. 3d 1423.

[19] *Shell Petroleum, Inc.* 2000-2 USTC ¶50,561; 46 FedCl 719; *Bristol-Myers Barceloneta, Inc. et al*, 106 Civil No. 97-2567CC (D. P.R.).

return information concerning unrelated third party taxpayers to determine whether the IRS's positions constituted disparate treatment as in *IBM*.[20]

¶63 Privacy Act

The Privacy Act of 1974[21] prohibits the unauthorized disclosure by government agencies of information about individuals contained in the agencies' systems of records, except insofar as these disclosures are within one or more of the exemptions provided by the law. The value of the Privacy Act is limited due to the blanket exclusion of a number of categories of information, including investigatory materials.[22] In addition, taxpayers are precluded from asserting a violation of the Privacy Act by virtue of Code Sec. 7852(e), which provides that the Privacy Act shall not be applied, directly or indirectly, to the determination of the existence or possible existence of liability for tax.[23]

An individual's right to access his own record maintained in a system of records must be determined under both the Privacy Act and the FOIA. An individual is entitled to the maximum access permissible under either statute when it comes to his or her own records.[24]

Compliance not required

Compliance with the Privacy Act is not a prerequisite to enforcement of an IRS summons.[25] In addition, a taxpayer must exhaust the administrative remedies under the FOIA (¶61) and Privacy Act before a suit can be maintained against the IRS for disclosure of documents.[26] However, to the extent that the IRS engages in the practice of collecting protected information unconnected to any investigation of past, present, or anticipated violations of statutes that it is authorized to enforce, the Privacy Act is violated, and, thus, documents must be disclosed.[27]

¶64 Taxpayer Bill of Rights

The Technical and Miscellaneous Revenue Act of 1988 (TAMRA)[28] contained a Taxpayer Bill of Rights. The Taxpayer Bill of Rights gave taxpayers various rights in dealing with the IRS, provided procedures for taxpayers regarding the IRS, added levy and lien provisions, and extended the Tax Court's jurisdiction (¶42). The IRS is required to disclose these rights to taxpayers. Among the key rights are:

1. Disclosure of rights to taxpayers;

---

[20] *International Business Machines Corp. v. U.S.*, ClsCt, 65-1 USTC ¶15,629, 343 F2d 914 (*cert. denied* 382 US 1082).

[21] 5 U.S.C. §552a(b); P.L. 93-579.

[22] Douglas H. Walter, "Changes in Strategic Positions Between the IRS and Tax Practitioners: Impact of the Disclosure of Information," 58 TAXES—*The Tax Magazine* 825.

[23] *Rosenberger*, DC Iowa, 86-1 USTC ¶9194; *Warden*, DC Tex., 86-2 USTC ¶9507.

[24] 625 U.S.C. §552a(t). See H.R. Rep. No. 98-726, 98th Cong., 2d Sess., pt. 2, at 16-17 (1984); Internal Revenue Manual 1.3.13.3.9(3).

[25] *McAnlis*, CA-11, 84-1 USTC ¶9187; 721 F2d 334, cert. den., 104 SCt 2681; *Uhrig*, DC Md., 84-2 USTC ¶9694; *Dennis*, DC Ill., 87-1 USTC ¶9323; *Dennis*, DC Ill., 87-2 USTC ¶9468.

[26] *Lilienthal v. Parks*, DC Ark., 83-1 USTC ¶9396.

[27] *Clarkson*, CA-11, 82-2 USTC ¶9437, 678 F2d 1368.

[28] Technical and Miscellaneous Revenue Act of 1988 (P.L. 100-647).

2. Establishment of standards for determining whether the selection of time and place for interviewing a taxpayer is reasonable;

3. Abatement of penalties when taxpayers act on erroneous advice by the IRS;

4. Issuance of a Taxpayer Assistance Order when taxpayers are about to suffer a hardship;

5. Expiration of temporary regulations after three years;

6. Payment of taxes on the installment basis by written agreement;

7. Recourse when the IRS intentionally disregards the Code or regulations in connection with the collection of tax; and

8. Prohibits disclosure or use by a tax return preparer of information furnished for preparation of a return for other purposes.

Disclosure of taxpayer rights

A statement using simple and nontechnical terms and explaining the rights of a taxpayer and the obligations of the IRS during the audit, appeals, refund, and collection processes must be distributed to all taxpayers the IRS contacts with respect to the determination or collection of any tax.

Interviewing standards

The IRS must disclose standards for determining whether the selection of a time and place for interviewing a taxpayer is reasonable. Either the taxpayer or the IRS may, with advance notice, make an audio recording of the interview. If the IRS does, it must provide a transcript or copy at cost to the taxpayer upon request. A taxpayer is entitled to be represented during an interview.[29]

Erroneous written advice

The IRS must abate any portion of any penalty or addition to tax attributable to erroneous advice furnished to the taxpayer in writing by an IRS officer or employee in response to a specific written request by the taxpayer. However, the portion of the penalty or addition to tax may not be the result of a failure by the taxpayer to provide adequate or accurate information.[30]

Taxpayer Assistance Orders

Upon application by the taxpayer to the Office of the National Taxpayer Advocate a Taxpayer Assistance Order may be issued if it is determined that the taxpayer is suffering or is about to suffer a significant hardship as a result of how the internal revenue laws are being administered (see ¶106).

Expiration of temporary regulations

All temporary regulations (¶72) issued after November 20, 1988, must also be issued as proposed regulations (¶73). Any temporary regulation will expire within three years after issuance.[31]

---

[29] Code Sec. 7521.
[30] Code Sec. 6404(f).

[31] Code Sec. 7805(e).

¶64

Installment payment agreements

The IRS may enter into a written agreement with a taxpayer allowing payment of taxes on an installment basis if it will facilitate collection. The IRS Restructuring and Reform Act of 1998 requires the IRS to enter into installment agreements in certain cases.[32]

The agreement may be altered, modified, or terminated if the taxpayer fails to make timely payment of any installment or any other tax liability or to provide a financial condition update upon request by the IRS. The Taxpayer Bill of Rights 2 (1996) requires the IRS to notify the taxpayer 30 days before any such change to an installment agreement.[33]

Intentional disregard of regulations

Taxpayers may sue the IRS for reckless or intentional disregard of the IRC (¶22) or regulations in connection with the collection of a tax (¶71). An action must be commenced in federal district court (¶43) within two years after the date when the right of action has accrued.[34]

Disclosure by tax return preparer

Disclosure or use by a tax return preparer of information furnished for preparation subjects the preparer to a penalty of $250 per disclosure, not to exceed $10,000. A tax return preparer, for this purpose, includes anyone who is in the tax return preparation business, provides services in connection with tax return preparation, or prepares returns for compensation. This penalty is not imposed if disclosure is pursuant to a Code provision permitting disclosure or pursuant to a court order (¶65).[35]

¶65 Disclosure Exemptions

The IRS is required to delete seven categories of confidential information before making any written determination or background file document available for public inspection. The first category includes names, addresses, and other identifying details of the person to whom the ruling pertains and of additional persons other than those making "third-party contacts."[36]

The other six categories are the same as the exceptions that are set out in the FOIA. These exemptions include the following:

1. Information to be kept secret for national defense or foreign policy reasons under criteria set out by Executive Order (¶95) and which is properly classified;

2. Information exempt from disclosure under any other statute;

3. Trade secrets and commercial or financial information that is given to the IRS by a third party and privileged or confidential in nature;

---

[32] Code Sec. 6159(c).
[33] Code Sec. 6159(b)(5).
[34] Code Sec. 7433.

[35] Code Sec. 6713.
[36] Code Sec. 6110(c).

4. Information the disclosure of which would be an unwarranted invasion of personal privacy;

5. Matters contained in or related to various reports prepared by or for the use of an agency responsible for the regulation or supervision of financial institutions; and

6. Geological and geophysical information and data, including maps, concerning wells.

Background file documents

In addition, the IRS is not required to disclose any general written determination (¶80) and related background file document relating to the IRS Commissioner's approval of adoption or change of the following:[37]

1. A taxpayer's annual accounting period;[38]

2. A taxpayer's method of accounting;[39]

3. A partner or partnership's tax year;[40] and

4. The funding method of a qualified pension plan.[41]

¶66 Public Inspection and Copying of Documents

The Administrative Procedure Act (APA) (¶25) requires federal agencies, including the IRS, to make other important decisions and documents available for public inspection and copying.[42] Each agency, in accordance with published rules, must provide public access to the following documents:[43]

1. Final opinions, including concurring and dissenting opinions, as well as orders, made in the adjudication of cases;

2. Those statements of policy and interpretations that have been adopted by the agency and are not published in the *Federal Register* (¶51); and

3. Administrative staff manuals and instructions to staff that affect a member of the public.

4. Copies of all records, regardless of form or format, which have been released to any person under the FOIA and which, because of the nature of their subject matter, the agency determines have become or are likely to become the subject of subsequent requests for substantially the same records; and

5. A general index of the records referred to in 4.

If the materials are promptly published and copies offered for sale, these rules do not apply, however.

---

[37] Code Sec. 6110(g)(5)(B).
[38] Code Sec. 442.
[39] Code Sec. 446(e).
[40] Code Sec. 706.

[41] Code Sec. 412.
[42] 5 U.S.C. §552.
[43] 5 U.S.C. §552(a)(2).

Notification of noncompliance and right to appeal

An agency must determine within 10 business days after the receipt of a request for records whether to comply and must immediately notify the person making such request of its determination, the reasons therefore, and of the right to appeal any adverse decision.[44] In the event of an appeal, an agency must make a determination within 20 business days after the receipt of such appeal and, if the denial of the request for records is upheld, must notify the person making such request of the provisions for judicial review by the proper U.S. District Court.[45] Some records, such as those compiled for law enforcement purposes, are excluded from coverage under the APA.[46]

¶67 Electronic Freedom of Information Act

The Freedom of Information Act was amended by the "Electronic Freedom of Information Act Amendments of 1996," generally requiring U.S. government agencies, including the IRS, to make records available electronically. Under these provisions a clearly unwarranted invasion of personal privacy, should be prevented by deleting identifying details. However, the justification for the deletion should be explained and the extent of any deletion should be indicated.[47]

Subsequent legislation imposed specific electronic reporting requirements on the IRS. The IRS is required to establish procedures for all tax forms, instructions, and publications to be made available electronically on the Internet in a searchable database. These items are to be placed on the Internet at approximately the same time that the paper versions are available to the public. The provision also requires the IRS to make "other taxpayer guidance" available electronically on the Internet in a searchable database at approximately the same time such guidance is available to the public in paper form. The law did not spell out what other types of taxpayer guidance need to be posted on the internet.[48]

The IRS is required to make any Chief Counsel advice that is available for public inspection also available by computer telecommunications within one year after issuance.[49]

Further, the IRS is required to develop procedures not later than December 31, 2006 under which a taxpayer filing returns electronically can review the taxpayer's account electronically. The ability to electronically review also should apply to anyone designated by a taxpayer under Code Sec. 6103(c). However, the December 31, 2006 target date is subject to the condition that all necessary privacy safeguards are also in place by that date.[50]

---

[44] 5 U.S.C. § 552(a)(6)(A)(i).

[45] 5 U.S.C. § 552(a)(6)(A)(ii) and (a)(4)(B).

[46] See 5 U.S.C. § 552(b) for a complete listing of exceptions.

[47] The Freedom of Information Act, 5 U.S.C. § 552, as amended by Public Law No. 104-231, 110 Stat.

3048. Requirement is generally applicable to records created on or after November 1, 1996.

[48] Act Sec. 2003(d) of the IRS Restructuring and Reform Act of 1998 (P.L. 105-206).

[49] Act Sec. 3509(d)(4) of P.L. 105-206.

[50] Act Sec. 2005 of P.L. 105-206.

Internet

A U.S. government website, *http://www.irs.gov/*, is designed to provide one-stop access to all federal government online information and services. Information on the website is arranged in several different ways. For example information is categorized by type of user or tax specialty:

(1) individuals

(2) businesses

(3) charities & non-profits

(4) government entities

(5) tax professionals and

(6) retirement plans.

The IRS website contains links to most IRS communications that the IRS also makes available in print. Following is a partial listing of IRS documents available on the Internet:

Internal Revenue Bulletins (see ¶52).

Advance Notice for Tax Professionals. The IRS often releases revenue rulings, revenue procedures, and other technical tax items in advance of publishing them in the Internal Revenue Bulletin (IRB). The full contents of these advance items (or "early drops") are available for retrieval.

Forms and Publications (see ¶102). Forms with instructions, publications and notices. Includes "Fill-in forms" which allow a taxpayer to enter information while the form is displayed and then print the completed form.

Tax Law Issues, Nibbles & Bytes. Includes a tax calendar, collection financial standards, applicable federal rates, and other hot tax professional questions.

IRS E-file. Information for taxpayers filing electronically including information on electronic payment options.

Abusive Tax Shelters. In recent years, the IRS has identified a number of abusive tax shelter plans being sold by tax shelter promoters. These plans are not in conformance with Tax Code requirements and have been disallowed by the IRS. Abusive Tax Shelters points out some of the red flags that might be present in a plan under consideration.

Income Tax Treaties. The United States and certain other nations have entered into treaties affecting the mutual application of each nation's tax laws. This page links to the complete texts of U.S. Income Tax Treaties.

Market Segment Specialization Program Audit Techniques Guides (¶95). Audit Techniques guides for various market segments are available from this site.

Tax Regulations (¶71). List of tax regulations issued since August 1, 1995, with references to plain language summaries where available. This list also provides a way to comment on regulations with an open comment period.

Federal Register. Find Federal laws, regulations, proposed rules and notices, upcoming Federal Register issues; and Executive orders, proclamations and other Presidential documents.

Tax Relief in Disaster Situations. If a taxpayer has been impacted by a federally declared disaster, the disaster services page may be helpful.

Electronic Reading Room

This link enables electronic access to federal agency records without a formal FOIA request. Included on this link are:

(1) **Published Tax Guidance**

- Advance Releases—early distribution of some I.R.B. materials before they are published in the I.R.B.,
- Final (see ¶71), Temporary (see ¶72), and Proposed (see ¶73) IRS Regulations,
- IRS Publications (see ¶101),
- Notices (see ¶79), and
- Internal Revenue Bulletins (see ¶52).

(2) **Administrative Manuals & Instructions**

- *Chief Counsel (CC) Notices* (see ¶78),
- *Internal Revenue Manual* (IRM) (see ¶76), and
- *LMSB Industry Director Guidance* (see ¶98).

(3) **Program Plans & Reports**

- *Annual Performance Plan*—high level programs and services the IRS carries out to accomplish its mission, goals, and strategies outlined in its strategic plan;
- *FOIA Annual Reports*—provides detailed information concerning the IRS administration of the Freedom of Information Act;
- *IRS Strategic Plan* (see ¶34);
- *Priority Guidance Plan*—the guidance priority list (or Business Plan) identifies and prioritizes the tax issues that should be addressed through regulations, rulings, and other published administrative guidance; and
- *Privacy Impact Assessments*—the IRS conducts a Privacy Impact Assessment (PIA) on information systems collecting personally identifiable information from the public. The PIAs ensure that: the public is aware of the information that is collected about them, that any impact these systems have on personal privacy is adequately addressed, and that only enough personal information is collected to administer IRS programs, and no more.
- *Treasury Inspector General for Tax Administration* Annual Audit Plans (TIGTA) (see ¶38).

(4) **Non-precedential Rulings & Advice**

- Actions on Decisions (AOD) (see ¶93),
- Appeals Settlement Guidelines (see ¶99),
- Chief Counsel Bulletins (see ¶96),
- Exempt Organization Field Memoranda (see ¶82),

¶67

- General Counsel Memoranda (see ¶92),
- Information Letters (see ¶99),
- IRS Written Determinations (see ¶82) (Private Letter Ruling (PLR) (see ¶81), Technical Advice Memorandum (TAM) (see ¶86), and Chief Counsel Advice (CCA) (see ¶96), and
- Legal Advice Issued by Field Attorneys (see ¶97).

(5) **Training & Reference Materials**

- *Advance Pricing Agreement (APA) Training Materials* (see ¶62);
- *Appeals Coordinated Issues* (ACI)—an ACI is an issue or category of cases of IRS-wide impact or importance that requires Appeals' coordination to ensure uniformity and consistency nationwide.
- *Chief Counsel Advice (CCA) Training Materials* (see ¶66);
- *Disclosure Litigation Reference Book*—the primary Disclosure laws that impact the IRS are covered;
- *EO Tax Law Training Articles* (see ¶82);
- *Market Segment Specialization Program* (Audit Techniques Guides) (see ¶95), and
- *Technical Training Program for Businesses*—special training courses available to IRS auditors.

¶67

Chapter 8
Official IRS Positions

¶70 Overview

The Administrative Procedure Act (APA) (¶25) defines "agency" as each authority of the Government of the United States, whether or not it is within or subject to review by another agency.[1] Thus, promulgation of a rule by the IRS is governed by APA requirements.

A "rule" is defined as the whole or a part of an agency statement of general or particular applicability and future effect designed to implement, interpret, or prescribe law or policy or describing the organization, procedure, or practice requirements of an agency.[2] This definition applies to regulations (¶71), revenue rulings (¶74), revenue procedures (¶75), advance rulings and determinations (¶80), and other official IRS documents (¶76-79).

For purposes of determining whether action by an agency is within rulemaking authority," rulemaking" involves the promulgation of concrete proposals, declaring generally applicable policies binding on the affected public generally, but not adjudicating the rights and obligations of the parties before it.[3] Rulemaking, which is legislative in nature, is primarily concerned with policy considerations for the future rather than evaluation of past conduct, and looks not to evidentiary facts but to policy-making conclusions to be drawn from the facts.[4]

APA requirements directly affect the administration and enforcement of federal tax law by the IRS. The APA is the legal authority for rulemaking and promulgation of procedures necessary to insure fairness and equity in administration of the federal income tax laws.

In this context, the IRS issues numerous official positions, including final regulations (¶71), temporary regulations (¶72), proposed regulations (¶73), revenue rulings (¶74), revenue procedures (¶75), Internal Revenue Manual (¶76), Commissioner delegation orders (¶77), Chief Counsel orders and notices (¶78), and other announcements and notices (¶79).

Paragraphs 71-79 describe each type of IRS position. Issues concerning the degree of reliance and their retroactive application are discussed at .05 and .10, respectively, of each paragraph.

¶71 Final Regulations and Treasury Decisions

Regulations are authorized by Code Sec. 7805 and explain the IRS's position, prescribe operation rules, and provide the mechanics for compliance with the

---

[1] 5 U.S.C. § 551(1).
[2] 5 U.S.C. § 551(4).

[3] *PBW Stock Exchange, Inc. v. Securities and Exchange Commission*, CA-3, 485 F2d 718 (cert. denied 416 US 969).
[4] *American Express Co. v. U.S.*, 473 F2d 1050.

various federal income tax laws (see sample at ¶120).[5] This, according to some authorities on administrative law, is an authorization to promulgate interpretative regulations, authority the Treasury Secretary probably would have without the specific IRC provision. Thus, it is not to be inferred from Code Sec. 7805 that all regulations are legislative regulations. Regulations have generally been classified into three broad categories: legislative; interpretative; and procedural. As to reliance and retroactivity, see .05 and .10, below.

Legislative regulations

Legislative regulations are those for which the IRS is specifically authorized by the Internal Revenue Code to prescribe the operational rules. Generally, legislative regulations have the force and effect of law. However, when legislative regulations have been promulgated without publication in conformance with the Administrative Procedure Act[6], exceed the scope of the IRS's delegated power[7], are contrary to law[8], or are unreasonable, courts have considered them to have no force and effect.[9]

Interpretative regulations

Interpretative regulations, as the name implies, explain the IRS's position on the various sections of the Internal Revenue Code. Although interpretative regulations do not have the force and effect of law, the courts often accord them substantial weight. Various theories have evolved in the courts to test the validity or weight to be accorded interpretative regulations (¶46).

Procedural regulations

Procedural regulations are considered to be directive, rather than mandatory, and, thus, do not have the force and effect of law.[10] Some administrative law authorities consider procedural regulations, which are designed to govern an agency's own proceedings, to be legislative rules, whether or not specific power is given to issue such rules.

Treasury Decisions

When regulations are issued in final, permanent form, they are promulgated by a document called a Treasury Decision (T.D.) (see sample at ¶120). By way of distinction, the term "regulation" has come to be restricted to the provisions of the organized bodies of regulations and the term "Treasury Decision" to the instructions and interpretations issued by the IRS Commissioner with the approval of the Treasury Secretary.

A Treasury Decision includes a preamble statement that describes the contents of the new final or proposed regulation in a manner sufficient to apprise a reader who is not an expert in the subject area of the general subject matter of the

---

[5] Code Sec. 7805(a).

[6] *American Standard, Inc.*, CtCls, 79-2 ustc ¶9417, 602 F2d 256.

[7] *Panama Refining Co. v. Ryan*, SCt, 293 US 388.

[8] *M.E. Blatt Co. v. U.S.*, SCt, 38-2 ustc ¶9599, 305 US 267.

[9] *Joseph Weidenhoff, Inc.*, 32 TC 1222, CCH Dec. 23,761 (Acq.).

[10] *Luhring v. Glotzbach*, CA-4, 62-2 ustc ¶9547, 304 F2d 560.

¶71

rulemaking document. The promulgation date of a regulation or Treasury Decision is the date the document is filed by the *Federal Register* for public inspection.[11] Such regulations are effective for the period covered by the law section they interpret unless they specifically provide otherwise.

Code of Federal Regulations

Regulations follow the numbered sequence of the Internal Revenue Code. Title 26 of the Code of Federal Regulations pertains to the Internal Revenue Code, and Part 1 of Title 26 relates to federal income tax. Thus, in the numbering system for regulations, income tax regulations are preceded by the number "¶1" and followed by the applicable Internal Revenue Code section. For example, the regulations section on qualified pension, profit sharing, and stock bonus plans is designated "Reg. § 1.401-1." Similarly, Part 20 of Title 26 pertains to estate tax, Part 25 to gift tax, Part 31 to withholding of income tax, Part 301 to procedure and administration, and Part 601 to the statement of procedural rules (¶75).

Reliance

Regulations and Treasury Decisions on matters of administration or procedure or exercising a discretion conferred by statute have the force and effect of law and are binding upon the taxpayer to the same extent as the statute itself.[12] However, an administrative practice contrary to, or not consistent with, a statute is without legal effect and, generally, will be disregarded by the courts.[13] Therefore, an erroneous interpretation of the law does not prevent the IRS from asserting an appropriate tax, even though a taxpayer may have been misled by the interpretation expressed in a regulation.[14]

Unless Congress clearly indicates to the contrary, reenactment of a statutory provision that has received a long-continued administrative construction is deemed to have been adopted by Congress.[15] Similarly, where Congress has full knowledge of a departmental construction of a statute and is aware of an insistence for a change but declines to make the change and also reenacts the statute, the effect of reenactment is a congressional adoption of the departmental construction.[16]

However, almost no weight will be given to a departmental construction that is an enlargement of a statute, is not uniform, and is not long-continued.[17] Therefore, the doctrine of statutory incorporation of a prior administrative ruling by reenactment of a statute without substantial change will not apply where the regulation has been in effect only a short time before such reenactment and there is no positive proof that Congress had prior knowledge of the regulation.[18]

---

[11] Rev. Rul. 56-517, 1956-2 CB 966.

[12] *Stegall v. Thurman*, DC, 175 F. 813.

[13] *Morill v. Jones*, 106 US 466; *Robinson v. Lundrigan*, 27 US 173.

[14] *Langstaff v. Lucas*, CA-6, 1 USTC ¶188, 13 F2d 1022.

[15] *Winmill*, SCt, 38-2 USTC ¶9550, 305 US 79; *Lykes v. U.S.*, SCt, 52-1 USTC ¶9259, 343 US 118.

[16] *Provost v. U.S.*, SCt, 1 USTC ¶153, 269 US 443.

[17] *Merritt v. Cameron*, 137 US 542; *U.S. v. Healy*, 160 US 136; *U.S. v. Detroit First Nat'l Bank*, 234 US 245; *Iselin v. U.S.*, 270 US 245.

[18] *Casey v. Sterling Cider Co.*, CA-1, 294 F. 426; *Sun Pipe Line Co.*, CA-3, 42-1 USTC ¶9371, 126 F2d 888.

Retroactivity

Generally final regulations are not effective before the earliest of the following dates:

> the date on which such regulation is filed with the Federal Register,
>
> the date any proposed or temporary regulation to which the final regulation relates was filed with the Federal Register, or
>
> the date on which any notice substantially describing the expected contents of the final regulation is issued to the public.

This general prohibition on retroactive regulations does not apply to any regulation relating to internal IRS policies, practices, or procedures and may be superseded by a legislative grant authorizing the IRS to prescribe the effective date with respect to a statutory provision. The IRS also may issue retroactive final regulations to correct a procedural defect in the issuance of a regulation or to prevent abuse. The IRS may provide that taxpayers may elect to apply a regulation retroactively from the date of publication of the regulation.[19]

Intentional disregard of regulations. The Taxpayer Bill of Rights,[20] provides that a taxpayer may sue the IRS for reckless or intentional disregard of the IRC or regulations in connection with the collection of a tax (¶64). An action must be commenced in federal district court (¶43) within two years after the date when the right of action has accrued.

¶72 Temporary Regulations

Temporary regulations are "adopted regulations" within the meaning of Code Sec. 7805(b) but are short-lived and are subsequently replaced by final regulations. Any temporary regulation will expire within three years after issuance (¶64).

All temporary regulations issued after November 20, 1988, must also be issued as proposed regulations (¶64). Although general notices for rulemaking (¶51) are not required for temporary regulations, the text of a temporary regulation may, at the discretion of the IRS, serve as the text for proposed rulemaking. Like final regulations, temporary regulations are promulgated by Treasury Decisions (¶71).

Reliance

Until final regulations have been issued, temporary regulations have the same force and effect of law as final regulations (¶71), and, thus, taxpayers may rely on them for planning tax transactions.

Retroactivity

Temporary regulations must have an effective date no earlier than the date of publication in the Federal Register or the date on which any notice substantially describing the expected contents of the regulation is issued to the public.

---

[19] Code Sec. 7805(b), as amended by P.L. 104-168 (Taxpayer Bill of Rights 2 (1996)). [20] Code Sec. 7433.

Any regulations filed or issued within 18 months of the enactment of the statutory provision to which the regulation relates may be issued with retroactive effect. This general prohibition on retroactive regulations may be superseded by a legislative grant authorizing the IRS to prescribe the effective date with respect to a statutory provision. The IRS may issue retroactive temporary regulations to prevent abuse. The IRS also may issue retroactive temporary regulations to correct a procedural defect in the issuance of a regulation. The IRS may provide that taxpayers may elect to apply a temporary regulation retroactively from the date of publication of the regulation. Final regulations may take effect from the date of publication of the temporary or proposed regulation to which they relate. These rules do not apply to any regulation relating to internal IRS policies, practices, or procedures.[21]

¶73 Proposed Regulations

Proposed regulations are prepared to provide timely guidance when delays inherent in the preparation of temporary or final regulations would be unwise or when additional input is required before a final position can be adopted by the IRS. All temporary regulations (¶72) issued after November 20, 1988, must also be issued as proposed regulations (¶64).

Although general notices for rulemaking (¶51) are not required for temporary regulations, general notices for proposed rulemaking (NPRM) are required for proposed regulations and are published in the *Federal Register* (¶51). Interested parties must be given an opportunity to participate in the rulemaking through submission of written data, views, or arguments. The deadline for comments is stated in the NPRM.

Generally, publication of a substantive rule must be made not less than 30 days before its effective date.[22] Therefore, interested parties must be given a minimum of 30 days in which to comment. Sometime thereafter, the proposed regulations are issued in final, permanent form. Finalization is promulgated by Treasury Decisions (¶71).

Reliance

Although proposed regulations provide guidance for tax planning, taxpayers may not ordinarily rely on them to support a tax position. Courts have generally determined that proposed regulations are not entitled to judicial deference, and carry no more weight than a position advanced on brief by one of the parties.[23]

On occasion, where a taxpayer has relied on a reasonable interpretation of a proposed regulation, the Tax Court has sustained the taxpayer's position. For example, when the Tax Court recently addressed the issue of reliance on proposed regulations in the context of a motion for summary judgment against a

---

[21] Code Sec. 7805(b).

[22] 5 U.S.C. §553.

[23] *Boyer,* 55 TCM 871, TC Memo. 1988-220, CCH Dec. 44,788(M); *Freesen,* 84 TC 920, CCH Dec. 42,098,

rev'd on other grounds CA-7, 86-2 USTC ¶9617, 798 F2d 195; *Natomas North America, Inc.,* 90 TC 710, CCH Dec. 44,700.

taxpayer claiming abuse of discretion concerning retroactive changes in proposed regulations, the court stated that the Treasury Department has the duty to avoid misleading taxpayers and should not be empowered retroactively to penalize taxpayers who acted "in reliance on the most reasonable interpretation."[24]

One Court of Appeals, in holding that items published by the IRS for information and guidance, including proposed regulations, do not bind the Commissioner regardless of the promises they contain, stated that whereregulations exist in proposed form, the taxpayer's wisest course would be to comply with the regulations' requirements even before their enactment in final form.[25] Two other Courts of Appeals disagreed, stating that since regulations are subject to change, even to substantial change, prior to final promulgation, strict compliance with proposed regulations could cause unnecessary extra time and labor, an unwarranted taxpayer burden.[26]

Retroactivity

Proposed regulations must have an effective date no earlier than the date of publication in the Federal Register or the date on which any notice substantially describing the expected contents of the regulation is issued to the public. Any regulations filed or issued within 18 months of the enactment of the statutory provision to which the regulation relates may be issued with retroactive effect. This general prohibition on retroactive regulations may be superseded by a legislative grant authorizing the IRS to prescribe the effective date with respect to a statutory provision. The IRS may issue retroactive proposed regulations to prevent abuse. The IRS also may issue retroactive proposed regulations to correct a procedural defect in the issuance of a regulation. The IRS may provide that taxpayers may elect to apply a proposed regulation retroactively from the date of publication of the regulation. Final regulations may take effect from the date of publication of the temporary or proposed regulation to which they relate. The provision does not apply to any regulation relating to internal IRS Department policies, practices, or procedures.[27]

¶74 Revenue Rulings

A revenue ruling is an official interpretation by the IRS of the internal revenue laws, related statutes, tax treaties, and regulations that has been published in the Internal Revenue Bulletin (¶52). It sets forth the conclusion of the IRS on how the tax law is applied to an entire set of facts. Revenue rulings are issued only by the IRS National Office and are published for the information and guidance of taxpayers, IRS officials, and other interested parties (see sample at ¶120).[28] (Advance rulings and determinations are discussed at ¶80-¶88.)

---

[24] American Bar Association, Section of Taxation, Letter submitted to the IRS, dated May 6, 1988, commenting on Reg. §1.704-1, Footnote no. 18; *Elkins*, 81 TC 669, CCH Dec. 40,514.

[25] *CWT Farms, Inc.*, CA-11, 85-1 USTC ¶9277, 755 F2d 790, *aff'g* 79 TC 1054.

[26] *LeCroy Research Systems Corp.*, CA-2, 85-1 USTC ¶9107, 751 F2d 123, *rev'g on other grounds* 47 TCM 1345, TC Memo. 1984-145, CCH Dec. 41,086(M); *Gehl Co.*, CA-7, 86-2 USTC ¶9530, 795 F2d 1324.

[27] Code Sec. 7805(b).

[28] Rev. Proc. 99-1, IRB 1999-1, 6; Rev. Proc. 89-14, 1989-1 CB 814.

Effect of issuance on prior rulings

Revenue rulings and revenue procedures (¶74 and 75) that have an effect on other documents use the following defined terms to describe that effect:[29]

Amplified

The term "amplified" describes a situation where no change is being made in a prior published position, but the prior position is being extended to apply to a variation of the fact situation set forth therein. Thus, if an earlier ruling held that a principle applied to A, and the new ruling holds that the same principle also applies to B, the earlier ruling is amplified.

Clarified

The term "clarified" is used in those instances where the language in a prior ruling is being made clear because the language has caused, or may cause, some confusion. It is not used where a position in a prior ruling is being changed.

Distinguished

The term "distinguished" describes a situation where a ruling mentions a previously published ruling and points out an essential difference between them.

Modified

The term "modified" is used where the substance of a previously published position is being changed. Thus, if a prior ruling held that a principle applied to A but not to B, and the new ruling holds that it applies to both A and B, the prior ruling is modified because it corrects a published position.

Obsoleted

The term "obsoleted" describes a previously published ruling that is not considered determinative with respect to future transactions. Obsoleted is most commonly used in a ruling that lists previously published rulings that are obsoleted because of changes in law or regulations. A ruling also may be obsoleted because the substance has been included in regulations subsequently adopted.

Revoked

The term "revoked" describes situations where the position in the previously published ruling is not correct and the correct position is being stated in the new ruling.

Superseded

The term "superseded" describes a situation where the new ruling does nothing more than restate the substance and situation of a previously published ruling. Thus, superseded is used to republish under the 1986 Code and regulations the same position published under the 1954 Code and regulations. Superseded also is used when there is a desire to republish in a single ruling a series of situations, names, and so forth, that were previously published over a period of time in separate rulings. If the new ruling does more than restate the substance of a prior ruling, a combination of terms is used. For example, *modified and superseded* describes a situation where the substance of a previously published ruling is being changed in part and is continued without

---

[29] 1998-52 I.R.B. 89.

change in part and there is a desire to restate the valid portion of the previously published ruling in a new ruling that is self-contained. In this case, the previously published ruling is first modified and then, as modified, is superseded.

Supplemented

The term "supplemented" is used in situations in which a list, such as a list of the names of countries, is published in a ruling and that list is expanded by adding further names in subsequent rulings. After the original ruling has been supplemented several times, a new ruling may be published that includes the list in the original ruling and the additions, and supersedes all prior rulings in the series.

Suspended

The term "suspended" is used in rare situations to show that the previous published rulings will not be applied pending some future action, such as the issuance of new or amended regulations, the outcome of cases in litigation, or the outcome of an IRS study.

Obsolete rulings policy and practices

The IRS reviews rulings published prior to 1953, prior to the inauguration of the "Revenue Ruling" series, primarily to identify and publish lists of those rulings which, although not specifically revoked or superseded, are not considered determinative with respect to future transactions.[30] Some of those rulings, published in various series, have been specifically revoked or superseded. However, according to the IRS, many others should not be considered determinative for various reasons, such as:

1. The ruling may be unnecessary because the issue has been covered by regulations;

2. The conclusion may not now be applicable because of amendment of the statute, revision of the regulations, application of court decisions, or similar factors; or

3. The ruling may not have precedent value because the factual situation no longer exists or is not sufficiently described to permit clear application of the current statute and regulations.

Publication of a revenue ruling by the IRS announcing that a particular prior revenue ruling is not determinative with respect to future transactions does not necessarily mean that the conclusion or the *underlying rationale* has no current applicability. If the regulation now clearly covers the issue involved, the regulation is determinative and the published ruling is no longer the appropriate authority. Since this is an ongoing program, failure to include any particular ruling in an early list is not a conclusive indication that the ruling is determinative with respect to future transactions.[31]

---

[30] Rev. Proc. 89-14, 1989-1 CB 814.

[31] Rev. Proc. 67-6, 1967-1 CB 576; Rev. Proc. 89-14, 1989-1 CB 814.

Reliance

Revenue rulings do not have the force and effect of regulations (¶71), but are published to provide precedents to be used in the disposition of other cases and may be cited and relied upon for that purpose.[32] Where revenue rulings provide guidance by stating a useful rule of thumb for compliance, such as the "one-year rule" for determining whether employment is indefinite or temporary,[33] the Tax Court has held that it isnot bound by such a mechanical test and will look at all of the facts and circumstances before making a determination.[34]

Generally, taxpayers may rely upon published revenue rulings in determining the tax treatment of their own transactions and need not request specific rulings applying the principles of a published revenue ruling to the facts of their particular cases. However, the IRS cautions taxpayers, IRS personnel, and others concerned against reaching the same conclusion in other cases, unless the facts and circumstances are substantially the same, and advises such parties to consider the effect of subsequent legislation, regulations, court decisions, and revenue rulings.

Retroactivity

A revenue ruling generally applies retroactively, unless it includes a specific statement indicating, under the authority of Code Sec. 7805(b) (see ¶71.10), the extent to which it is to be applied without retroactive effect. When revenue rulings revoke or modify rulings previously published, the authority of Code Sec. 7805(b) ordinarily is invoked to provide that the new rulings will not be applied retroactively to the extent that they have adverse tax consequences to taxpayers.[35] Retroactivity does not apply to a ruling relating to the qualification of a pension, annuity, profit sharing, stock bonus, or bond purchase plan.

The courts have refused to retroactively apply revenue rulings where the IRS abused its discretion under Code Sec. 7805(b) by inconsistent administration of provisions of the applicable revenue ruling.[36] However, the IRS is not prohibited from revoking a revenue ruling where such ruling was based on a mistake of law and retroactive application of the correct ruling is not an abuse of discretion.[37]

In fact, the IRS may not be bound by a prior administrative position even where there has been congressional acquiescence of previous revenue rulings,[38] or where the taxpayer was not fully or correctly informed as to the material facts upon which the ruling was based, or where there had been material changes in the law or in facts subsequent to the time of issuance of the original ruling.[39]

---

[32] Reg. §601.601(d); Rev. Proc. 89-14, 1989-1 CB 814.

[33] Rev. Rul. 60-189, 1960-1 CB 60, amplified by Rev. Rul. 83-82, 1983-1 CB 45, 46.

[34] *Basden*, 37 TCM 991, TC Memo. 1978-232, CCH Dec. 35,229(M); *Libbey, Jr.*, 55 TCM 1052, TC Memo. 1988-254, CCH Dec. 44,828(M).

[35] Rev. Proc. 89-14, 1989-1 CB 814.

[36] *Farmers' and Merchants' Bank*, CA-4, 73-1 USTC ¶9336, 476 F2d 406, *vacating* DC W.Va., 72-1 USTC ¶9380, 341 FSupp 929.

[37] *Automobile Club of Michigan*, SCt, 57-1 USTC ¶9593, 353 US 180.

[38] *Schuster*, CA-7, 86-2 USTC ¶9664, 800 F2d 672, *aff'g* 84 TC 764, CCH Dec. 42,054.

[39] *Stevens Bros. Foundation, Inc.*, CA-8, 63-2 USTC ¶9820, 324 F2d 633 (cert. denied 376 US 969).

Generally, the courts will refrain from challenging the exercise or nonexercise of the IRS's discretion, but its discretion is not absolute. Where the taxpayer justifiably relies upon good faith in a prior IRS revenue ruling, it has been held that the IRS should exercise its discretion in favor of the taxpayer in deciding whether to apply its changed ruling retroactively.[40]

¶75 Revenue Procedures

A revenue procedure is an official statement of procedure published in the Internal Revenue Bulletin (¶52) that either affects the rights or duties of taxpayers or other members of the public under the Internal Revenue Code and related statutes and regulations, or, although not necessarily affecting the rights and duties of the public, should be a matter of public knowledge (see sample at ¶120).[41]

Revenue procedures usually reflect the contents of internal management documents. The stated policy of the IRS is to publish as much of the internal management document or communication as is necessary for an understanding of the procedure. When publication of the substance of a revenue procedure is required, it will usually be accomplished by an amendment to the Statement of Procedural Rules, Title 26, Part 601 of the Code of Federal Regulations (¶71).[42]

A statement of IRS position on a substantive tax issue will not be included in a revenue procedure. Where it is intended to announce both a statement of IRS position on a substantive tax issue and a statement of internal practice or procedure, a revenue procedure and a revenue ruling (¶74) will be issued simultaneously.

Reliance

Revenue procedures are directive and not mandatory and, thus, a taxpayer has no vested right to the benefit of the procedures when the IRS deviates from its internal rules.[43] Consequently, reliance is not an issue.

Retroactivity

Revenue procedures are generally applicable prospectively only. Therefore, a taxpayer may rely on a newly issued revenue procedure if the taxpayer is not informed that the revenue procedure is to be applied retroactively.[44]

¶76 Internal Revenue Manual

The Internal Revenue Manual (IRM) is a compilation of instructions promulgated by the IRS for the guidance of its employees when administering the income tax laws (see sample at ¶120).[45] Procedures set forth in the IRM are not

---

[40] *Newman,* 33 TCM 219, TC Memo. 1974-45, CCH Dec. 32,469(M).

[41] Reg. §601.601(d); Rev. Proc. 89-14, 1989-1 CB 814.

[42] Reg. §601.601(d).

[43] *Luhring, Jr. v. Glotzbach,* CA-4, 62-2 USTC ¶9547, 304 F2d 560; *Rosenberg,* CA-10, 71-2 USTC ¶9727, 450

F2d 529; *Montgomery,* 65 TC 511, CCH Dec. 33,536; *Houlberg,* 50 TCM 1125, TC Memo. 1985-497, CCH Dec. 42,398(M).

[44] *Matson Navigation Co.,* 68 TC 847, CCH Dec. 34,615.

[45] Archie W. Parnell, Jr., "The Internal Revenue Manual: Its Utility and Legal Effect," 32 *Tax Lawyer* 687, No. 3, Spring 1979.

binding upon the IRS because the provisions do not have the effect of a rule of law and are not promulgated pursuant to any mandate or delegation of authority by Congress.[46]

Although the IRM does not have the force of law, the IRS Restructuring and Reform Act of 1998 codified certain collection procedures in the IRM requiring the IRS to investigate the status of property prior to levy.[47]

Reliance

Even though the IRM is not accorded any legal effect, it includes information with the following characteristics that is useful to taxpayers.[48]

1. It sets forth the IRS's position, even a tentative one, with regard to a particular issue;

2. It construes a particular provision of the Internal Revenue Code;

3. It clarifies the meaning of general terms found in particular provisions of the Internal Revenue Code;

4. It amplifies regulations, revenue rulings, or revenue procedures; and

5. It requires IRS employees in certain situations to deal with taxpayers in a specified manner.

Thus, the IRM can provide significant insight into the methods utilized for administering income tax laws. Some deference by taxpayers and the courts may be given to the IRS's interpretation of the Internal Revenue Code as stated in the IRM.

At least one court thinks that there is an exception to the general rule that the IRM is non-binding on the IRS. In 1999, the Sixth Circuit ruled that IRM provisions requiring the suspension of a civil investigation as soon as an agent has a firm indication of fraud were intended to protect the taxpayer's constitutional rights and, thus, their violation could justify the suppression of evidence of criminal acts where that evidence was obtained during a civil investigation.[49]

Retroactivity

The IRM is provided for guidance of IRS employees only. Thus, retroactive application is not an issue.

¶77 Commissioner Delegation Orders

The IRS Commissioner is authorized to compromise any civil or criminal case arising under the internal revenue laws, including cases involving taxes, as well as those involving interest and penalties.[50] This authority, with limitations, may be delegated to subordinates. Redelegation of authority is announced by

---

[46] *First Federal Savings and Loan Association of Pittsburgh v. Goldman,* DC Pa., 86-2 USTC ¶ 9624.

[47] Code Sec. 6331(j)

[48] Parnell, Jr., "Internal Revenue Manual," 695.

[49] *I.L. McKee,* CA-6, 99-2 USTC ¶ 50,867.

[50] Code Sec. 7122; Temporary Reg. § 301.7122-1T.

Commissioner Delegation Orders (CDOs) (see sample at ¶120) which are published in the *Federal Register* (¶51).[51]

Reliance

Although CDOs are procedural and, thus, reliance is not an issue, where authority has been properly delegated, compromise agreements made by subordinates are binding on the taxpayer and the IRS.

Retroactivity

The delegation of authority by CDOs is procedural. Therefore, retroactive application is not an issue.

¶78 Chief Counsel Orders and Notices

Chief Counsel Orders and Notices (¶79) contain the official policies and practices of the Office of Chief Counsel (¶35). Since the Chief Counsel is responsible for administering the IRS's revenue ruling and revenue procedure publication program, including the standards for style and format, for the preparation and appropriate referral for publication of revenue rulings (¶74) reflecting interpretations of substantive tax law, for determining whether procedures should be published as revenue procedures (¶75), and for the initiation, content, and appropriate referral for publication of revenue procedures,[52] official orders and notices can provide invaluable guidance and information for taxpayers.

Reliance

Although these orders and notices are procedural and have no legal effect, they provide insight into the interworkings of the IRS. Litigation regarding the disclosure of documents prepared by the Office of Chief Counsel has focused on whether intra-agency advice and policy was predecisional or final opinion (¶91). Publication of policies and practices facilitate fair administration of tax laws and assist taxpayers in accessing information that can assist them in planning their tax transactions.

Retroactivity

Chief Counsel Orders and Notices are procedural or informational. Thus, retroactive application is not an issue.

¶79 Announcements and Notices

Announcements and notices issued by the IRS may contain guidance of a substantive or procedural nature and are used when guidance is needed quickly (note: these may contain advance text of revenue rulings) (see samples at ¶120). They are published in the Internal Revenue Bulletin.

---

[51] Rev. Proc. 96-38, 1996-2 CB 300; see, *e.g.*, Commissioner Delegation Order No. 67 (Rev. 24), January 27, 1998.

[52] Rev. Proc. 89-14, 1989-1 CB 814.

Examples of notices

There are several types of notices issued by the Treasury Department (¶23 and ¶32) and the IRS (¶24 and ¶34). Examples of notices include:

1. Official Notices containing guidance of a substantive or procedural nature (see sample at ¶120);

2. Chief Counsel Notices (¶78);

3. Notice of Determination;

4. Notice of Hearing;

5. Notice of Open Meeting; and

6. Notice of Extension of Time for Comments.

Reliance

In response to requests for clarification of the status of expedited guidance under the Tax Reform Act of 1986, the IRS determined that notices and announcements containing substantive or procedural guidance can be relied on by taxpayers to the same extent as revenue rulings (¶74) and revenue procedures (¶75).[53]

Administrative pronouncements are included in the definition of "substantial authority" (¶81).[54] The term "administrative pronouncement" not only refers to revenue rulings (¶74) and revenue procedures (¶75), but also includes properly executed announcements and notices.

Retroactivity

Where announcements and notices can be relied on to the same extent as a revenue ruling, retroactive application is presumed (¶74). If relied on to the same extent as a revenue procedure, application is usually prospective only (¶75). If announcements or notices are used merely as information and guidance, retroactive application is not an issue.

---

[53] Rev. Rul. 90-91, 1990-2 CB 262.   [54] Reg. § 1.6662-4(d)(3)(iii).

Chapter 9
Advance Rulings and Determinations

¶80 Overview

Private letter rulings (¶81), determination letters (¶82), technical advice memoranda (¶83), as well as opinion letters (¶84), information letters (¶85), technical memoranda (¶86), outgoing Treasury letters (¶87), closing agreements (¶88), pre-filing agreements (¶89) and technical expedited advice (¶90), are routinely disclosed by the IRS through its Letter Rulings Program. The purpose of advance rulings and determinations is to provide a timely response to individuals and organizations as to their status for tax purposes and as to the tax effects of their acts or transactions.

Advantages

The IRS Letter Rulings Program is advantageous to both the IRS and the taxpayer.[1]

Taxpayer

1. Informs the taxpayer of the IRS's position, thereby enabling the taxpayer to make a determination of whether or not to consummate the contemplated transaction;

2. Enables the taxpayer to choose a course of action which will avoid future controversy and litigation with the IRS; and

3. Enables the taxpayer to properly report the transaction once consummated, thereby promoting voluntary compliance.

The IRS

1. A high degree of uniformity in the application of the law and regulations is attained, since all rulings on prospective transactions, other than those concerned with qualification of exempt organizations and employee benefit plans, are issued from the National Office;

2. Advance rulings tend to decrease the amount of litigation that the IRS otherwise would be involved in;

3. The rulings program constitutes a source of valuable information to the IRS by keeping it abreast of the kinds of transactions which are being consummated or considered by taxpayers; and

4. The work of the auditing agents is also simplified, since they need only verify that the facts of the consummated transaction correspond to the facts in the ruling.

---

[1] Rogovin, "Four R's," 765.

Nonissuance of letter rulings

The IRS will decline to issue advance rulings or determinations where requests include one of the following topics:

1. Areas involving inherently factual matters in which rulings or determination letters will not be issued;

2. Areas in which rulings and determination letters will "not ordinarily" be issued ("Not ordinarily" means that unique and compelling reasons must be demonstrated to justify a ruling in these areas); and

3. Areas in which the IRS is temporarily not issuing advance rulings and determinations because the matters are under extensive study.

The IRS annually issues a revenue procedure providing a list of specific issues for which rulings will not or may not be issued.[2]

Annual publication of letter ruling procedures

A revenue procedure, which provides procedures for issuing rulings, determination letters, information letters, and for entering into closing agreements on specific areas of the federal income tax laws, is published annually, as the first revenue procedure of the year (*e.g.*, Rev. Proc. 2004-1), to incorporate changes in the program. Among other things, this revenue procedure defines various advance rulings and determinations.[3]

Erroneous written advice

The IRS is required to abate any portion of any penalty or addition to tax attributable to erroneous advice furnished to the taxpayer in writing by an IRS officer or employee in response to a specific written request by the taxpayer (¶64). However, the portion of the penalty or addition to tax may not be the result of a failure by the taxpayer to provide adequate or accurate information.[4]

¶81 Private Letter Rulings

A private letter ruling (also referred to as "letter ruling" or "private ruling") is a written response issued to a taxpayer by the National Office that interprets and applies the tax laws to that taxpayer's specific set of facts (see sample at ¶120).[5] Inquiries by individuals and organizations regarding their status for tax purposes and the tax effects of their acts or transactions are submitted by means of letters to the IRS Commissioner (¶34). Letter rulings, issued under the general supervision of the Office of the Chief Counsel (¶35), may serve as manifestations of a pre-existing, underlying interpretation or as a medium through which the IRS can, on a case-by-case basis, develop or extend such an interpretation.[6]

---

[2] See Rev. Proc. 2004-3, IRB 2004-1, 114.
[3] See Rev. Proc. 2004-1, IRB 2004-1, 1.
[4] Reg. § 301.6404-3(a).
[5] Reg. § 301.6110-2(d).

[6] James P. Holden and Michael S. Novey, "Legitimate Uses of Letter Rulings Issued to Other Taxpayers—A Reply to Gerald Portney," 37 *Tax Lawyer* 337, No. 2, Winter 1984.

The issuance of a letter ruling will be considered under certain conditions when new tax laws have been enacted and regulations have not been adopted. These conditions are:

1. If an inquiry presents an issue on which the answer seems to be clear from an application of the provisions of the statute to the facts described, a ruling will be issued in accordance with usual procedures;

2. If an inquiry presents an issue on which the answer seems reasonably certain but not entirely free from doubt, a ruling will be issued only if it is established that a business emergency requires a ruling or that unusual hardship will result from failure to obtain a ruling;

3. If an inquiry presents an issue that cannot be reasonably resolved prior to the issuance of regulations, a ruling will not be issued;

4. In any case in which the taxpayer believes that a business emergency exists or that an unusual hardship will result from failure to obtain a ruling, he should submit with the request a separate letter setting forth the facts necessary for the IRS to make a determination regarding the emergency or hardship. The IRS will not deem a "business emergency" to result from circumstances within the control of the taxpayer.[7]

Gifts, private foundations, and tax-exempt organizations rulings

In income and gift tax matters and matters involving taxes imposed under Chapter 42 of the Internal Revenue Code concerning private foundations and other tax-exempt organizations, the National Office issues rulings on prospective transactions and on completed transactions before the return is filed.[8] Advance rulings are allowed for estate tax issues (see discussion at ¶82 under "Estate and gift tax matters"). However, rulings will not ordinarily be issued if the identical issue is present in a return of the taxpayer for a prior year which is under active examination or audit by any Regional Office of Appeals.

National Office conferences

A taxpayer is entitled, as a matter of right, to only one conference with respect to a ruling request in the National Office.[9] The conference is usually held at the branch level of the appropriate division office of the Chief Counsel's Office (¶35), after the branch has had an opportunity to study the case so that there can be a free and open discussion of the issues. Because a taxpayer has no right to appeal the action, there is no real advantage to requesting a conference before the IRS has had an opportunity to study the case.

Reliance

Publication of private letter rulings, as well as all "written determinations" (¶62), is required by Code Sec. 6110. Congress specifically determined that, unless the IRS provides otherwise, private letter rulings may not be used or cited

---

[7] Reg. § 601.201(b)(5).
[8] Reg. § 601.201(b).

[9] See Rev. Proc. 2004-1, IRB 2004-1, 1.

as precedent.[10] The intent of the IRS Letter Ruling Program (¶80) is that no taxpayer has any basis for reliance on a letter ruling issued to another taxpayer.[11]

Evidence. However, many courts have varied as to the weight given to the existence of a private ruling in determining the tax liability of another taxpayer. As early as 1962, the U.S. Supreme Court cited private letter rulings in support of its interpretation of a substantive provision of the Internal Revenue Code, stating that such rulings reveal the interpretation put upon the statute by the agency charged with the responsibility of administering the revenue laws.[12]

In other pre-Code Sec. 6110 cases, it also was held that private letter rulings are probative of what the "standard of equality and fairness" incorporated into Code Sec. 7805(b) required,[13] and that a private ruling issued to another taxpayer is relevant to the imposition of the negligence penalty.[14]

Trend. This trend has continued in post-Code Sec. 6110 cases. The leading case cited private letter rulings as evidence of IRS practice, while conceding that they possess no precedential value.[15] Shortly thereafter, other courts, also conceding that private letter rulings have no precedential force, found that they are helpful, in general, in ascertaining the position adopted by the IRS and in showing that the position has been regularly considered and applied by the IRS[16] and that they can be cited to show inconsistent treatment under the law.[17]

Persuasive authority. Because the IRS is unlikely to reverse itself once a position has been established, private letter rulings tend to be highly predictive of the conduct of both the National and District Offices.[18] Since, according to some tax experts, it appears that advance rulings and determinations may be cited by the IRS as persuasive authority, they are endowed with such a high degree of credibility that they are only slightly less persuasive than true precedent. Whether or not precedential, private letter rulings constitute a historical record of interpretations of the tax laws by employees of the agency responsible for the tax law's administration which a court may consider.[19]

Substantial authority. In determining whether there is "substantial authority," the IRS will consider the following authority:

1. Applicable provisions of the Internal Revenue Code (¶22) and other statutory provisions;

2. Final (¶71), temporary (¶72), and proposed regulations (¶73) construing such statutes;

3. Court cases;

---

[10] Code Sec. 6110(j)(3); Reg. §301.6110-7(b).

[11] Reg. §601.201(l)(1); Rev. Proc. 2004-1, IRB 2004-1, 1.

[12] *Hanover Bank v. Commissioner*, SCt, 62-1 USTC ¶9487, 369 US 672.

[13] *International Business Machines Corp. v. U.S.*, ClsCt, 65-1 USTC ¶15,629, 343 F2d 914 (*cert. denied* 382 US 1082).

[14] *Corelli*, 66 TC 220, CCH Dec. 33,803.

[15] *Rowan Companies v. U.S.*, SCt, 81-1 USTC ¶9479, 452 US 247.

[16] *Xerox Corp. v. U.S.*, CtCls, 81-2 USTC ¶9579, 656 F2d 659.

[17] *Estate of Blackford*, 77 TC 1246, CCH Dec. 38,477.

[18] Holden and Novey, "Legitimate Uses of Letter Rulings," p. 345.

[19] Ibid., p. 347.

¶81

4. Administrative pronouncements (¶79) (including revenue rulings (¶74) and revenue procedures (¶75));

5. Tax treaties and regulations thereunder, and Treasury Department and other official explanations of such treaties;

6. Congressional intent as reflected in committee reports (¶46) and statements of managers;

7. General Explanations of tax legislation prepared by the Joint Committee on Taxation (the Blue Book);

8. Private letter rulings (¶81) and technical advice memoranda (¶83) issued after October 31, 1976;

9. Actions on decisions (¶93) and general counsel memoranda (¶92) issued after March 12, 1981 (as well as general counsel memoranda published in pre-1955 volumes of the Cumulative Bulletin);

10. IRS information or press releases; and

11. Notices and announcements published in the Internal Revenue Bulletin.[20]

The substantial authority standard is less stringent than a "more likely than not" standard (that is, a greater than 50-percent likelihood of being upheld in litigation), but stricter than a reasonable basis standard (the standard that generally will prevent imposition of the penalty relating to negligence or intentional disregard of rules and regulations).[21] Thus, a position with respect to the tax treatment of an item that is arguable but fairly unlikely to prevail in court would satisfy a reasonable basis standard, but not the substantial authority standard.

Rulings or determination letters issued to the taxpayer, technical advise memoranda in which the taxpayer is named, and affirmative statements in a revenue agent's report for a prior tax year may constitute substantial authority for the treatment of an item by the taxpayer. However, these items are not substantial authority if there was a misstatement or omission of material fact or facts that subsequently develop that are materially different from the facts on which the determination was based, or the determination is revoked or modified.[22]

The IRS is required to issue a list of positions for which there is not substantial authority;[23] however, no such list has been issued. The purpose of this list is to assist taxpayers in deciding whether to disclose a position with respect to a given item in order to avoid the understatement penalty. However, inclusion of a position on this list is not conclusive as to whether substantial authority exists with respect to that position. Additionally, conclusions reached in treatises, legal periodicals, legal opinions or opinions of tax professionals do not constitute authority.[24]

---

[20] Reg. § 1.6662-4(d)(2).
[21] Reg. § 1.6662-4(d)(3)(iii).
[22] Reg. § 1.6662-4(d)(3)(iv).

[23] Code Sec. 6662(d)(2)(D).
[24] Reg. § 1.6662-4(d)(3)(iii).

Precedent versus authority. Some experts contend that the IRS has confused the terms "precedent" and "authority," with precedent being the narrower term and authority the broader.[25] There are at least three ways in which the IRS's past conduct might be considered precedential:[26]

1. The past conduct, if known, might be useful in predicting the IRS's future conduct;

2. Reference to the IRS's past conduct may be persuasive to it as it contemplates future action; and

3. Reference to the IRS's past conduct may be persuasive to some other entity.

Retroactivity

A private letter ruling, except to the extent incorporated in a closing agreement (¶88), may be revoked or modified at any time under appropriate circumstances. If a ruling is revoked or modified, the revocation or modification applies to all years open under the statutes, unless the IRS Commissioner (¶34) or the Commissioner's delegate (¶77) exercises the discretionary authority under Code Sec. 7805(b) to limit the retroactive effect of the revocation or modification.[27]

Guidelines for retroactive application. The IRS has stated that, except in rare or unusual circumstances, revocation of a ruling issued to a taxpayer whose tax liability was directly involved will be prospective only, provided that:

1. There has been no misstatement or omission of material facts;

2. The facts subsequently developed are not materially different from the facts on which the ruling was based;

3. There has been no change in the applicable law;

4. The ruling was originally issued with respect to a prospective or proposed transaction; and

5. The taxpayer directly involved in the ruling acted in good faith in reliance upon the ruling and the retroactive revocation would be to his detriment.[28]

Reliance factor. Under these guidelines, reliance is the key factor if the facts have been properly stated.[29] The courts have shown a willingness to review the revocation of private letter rulings to determine whether the IRS abused its discretion. Where the IRS announces a change in policy and applies that policy indiscriminately, there is no basis for reliance and, thus, no abuse of discretion.[30]

---

[25] Timothy J. McCormally, "The Devil Citing Scripture: Reflections on Taxpayers' Use of Private Letter Rulings," 36 *The Tax Executive* 263, April 1984; Holden and Novey, "Legitimate Uses of Letter Rulings," 337.

[26] Holden and Novey, "Legitimate Uses of Letter Rulings," 344.

[27] Reg. §601.201(l)(1); Rev. Proc. 2004-1, IRB 2004-1, 1.

[28] Reg. §601.201(l)(5); Rev. Proc. 2004-1, IRB 2004-1, 1

[29] Nolan and Thuronyi, "Retroactive Application of Changes," 779.

[30] *Automobile Club of Michigan*, 57-1 USTC ¶9593, 353 US 180.

However, the courts have treated the IRS's discretion to be limited and have held the IRS strictly to the published standards.[31]

Disclosure of material facts. Most disputes concerning retroactive revocations of private letter rulings focus on whether the taxpayer has disclosed all material facts. Retroactive revocations have been upheld where the taxpayer failed to disclose subsequently developed material facts.[32] However, the courts have found that there is an abuse of discretion by the IRS in retroactively revoking a ruling where the material facts are sufficiently disclosed and where the consequences of retroactivity are harsh.[33]

¶82 Determination Letters

A determination letter is a written statement issued by a District Director in response to a written inquiry by a taxpayer that applies the principles and precedents previously announced by the National Office to a specific set of facts. Determination letters are issued only when a determination can be made on the basis of clearly established rules in the statute or regulations, or by a position in a ruling, opinion, or court decision published in the Internal Revenue Bulletin (¶52) that specifically answers the question presented.[34] Novel issues will not be considered. A determination letter does not include assistance provided by the U.S. competent authority pursuant to the mutual agreement procedure in tax treaties.[35]

Exempt Organizations

In exempt organizations matters, the Exempt Organizations Determinations office issues determination letters involving[36]

(1) Qualification for exempt status of organizations described in Code Secs. 501 and 521;[37]

(2) Classification of private foundation status;[38]

(3) Recognition of unusual grants to certain organizations;[39]

(4) Requests for relief in connection with applications for recognition of exemption;[40]

(5) Advance approval under Code Sec. 4945 of organizations' grant making procedures whose determination letter requests or applications disclose (or who have otherwise properly disclosed) a grant program or plans to conduct such a program;[41]

---

[31] *Lansons, Inc.,* CA-5, 80-2 USTC ¶9506, 622 F2d 774.

[32] *Stevens Bros. Foundation, Inc.,* 39 TC 93, CCH Dec. 25,708, aff'd in part and rev'd in part, CA-8, 63-2 USTC ¶9820, 324 F2d 633, cert. denied, 376 US 969; *Wisconsin Nipple and Fabricating Corp.,* 67 TC 490, CCH Dec. 34,153, aff'd, CA-7, 78-2 USTC ¶9606, 581 F2d 1235.

[33] *Lesavoy Foundation,* CA-3, 57-1 USTC ¶9229, 238 F2d 589, rev'g 25 TC 924, CCH Dec. 21,550.

[34] Reg. § 601.201(b).

[35] See Rev. Proc. 2002-52, IRB 2002-31, 242.

[36] Rev. Proc. 2004-4, IRB 2004-1, 75.

[37] To the extent provided in Rev. Proc. 90-27, 1990-1 C.B. 514.

[38] As provided in Rev. Proc. 76-34, 1976-2 C.B. 656.

[39] Under Code Secs. Code Sec. 170(b)(1)(A)(vi) and 509(a)(2).

[40] Under § 301.9100-1 of the Procedure and Administration Regulations.

[41] If questions arise regarding grant-making procedures that cannot be resolved on the basis of law,

(6) Whether certain organizations are excepted from filing annual information returns;[42]

(7) Whether certain organizations qualify as exempt operating foundations;[43] and

(8) Advance approval of voter registration activities.[44]

The Director, Exempt Organizations, periodically sends memoranda to the Director, Exempt Organizations Examination and all Area Managers to highlight recent developments in the law.

Since 1977, the Exempt Organizations Division has annually published a series of articles of interest to tax-exempt organizations, currently known as the Exempt Organizations Continuing Professional Education Technical Instruction Program.

Plan qualifications

The IRS annually issues procedures for obtaining determination letters involving the qualified status of pension, profit-sharing, stock bonus, annuity and employee stock ownership plans under (Code Secs. Code Secs. 401, 403(a), 409, and 4975(e)(7)), and the status for exemption of any related trusts or custodial accounts under Code Sec. 501(a).[45]

Income and gift tax matters

In income and gift tax matters, district directors issue determination letters in response to taxpayers' written requests on completed transactions that affect returns over which they have examination jurisdiction. Normally, determination letters are not issued on the tax consequences of proposed transactions. However, a district director may issue a determination letter on the replacement, even though not yet made, of involuntarily converted property under Code Sec. 1033 , if the taxpayer has filed an income tax return for the year in which the property was involuntarily converted.[46]

Estate and gift tax matters

District Directors issue determination letters regarding estate tax returns of decedents that will be audited by their offices but only if the answer to the questions presented are specifically covered by statute, Treasury Decision (¶71), or regulation (¶71). They do not issue determination letters on matters concerning the application of the estate tax to the prospective estate of a living person. In generation-skipping transfer tax matters, district directors issue determination letters in response to written requests affecting the generation-skipping transfer tax returns over which the district directors have examination jurisdiction. They

---

(Footnote Continued)

regulations, a clearly applicable revenue ruling, or other published precedent, EO Determinations will forward the matter to EO Technical for technical advice.

[42] Under Code Sec. 6033 as provided in Rev. Procs. 83-23, and 95-48, 1995-2 C.B. 418.

[43] As described in Code Sec. 4940(d).

[44] As described in Code Sec. 4945(f).

[45] Reg. §601.201(b), Rev. Proc. 2004-6, I.R.B. 2004-1, 197.

[46] Rev. Proc. 2004-1, IRB 2004-1, 1.

do not issue determination letters on matters concerning the application of the generation-skipping transfer tax before the distribution or termination takes place.[47]

Employment and excise tax matters

District Directors issue determination letters to taxpayers who have filed or who are required to file returns over which they have audit jurisdiction, but only if the answers to the questions are specifically covered by statute, Treasury Decision (¶ 71), or regulation (¶ 71). Because of the impact of these taxes upon the business operation of the taxpayer and because of special problems of administration both to the IRS and the taxpayer, District Directors may take appropriate action with regard to such requests, whether they relate to completed or prospective transactions or to returns previously filed or to be filed. Requests for a determination of employment status (Form SS-8) from taxpayers (other than federal agencies and instrumentalities) must be submitted to the appropriate IRS office listed on the current Form SS-8 and not directly to the national office.[48]

Nonissuance of determination letters

Determination letters will not be issued if:

1. It appears that the taxpayer has directed a similar inquiry to the National Office;
2. The same issue involving the same taxpayer is pending in a case before an Appeals Office;
3. The determination letter is requested by an industry, trade association, or similar group; or
4. The request involves an industry-wide problem.[49]

A determination letter will not be issued unless it is clearly shown that the request concerns a return that has been filed or is required to be filed and over which the district director has, or will have, examination jurisdiction.[50]

Reliance

Determination letters have the same force and effect as private letter rulings (¶ 81).

Retroactivity

Determinations may be revoked by a District Director upon re-examination of a taxpayer's return. Revocation is automatically retroactive if the determination concerns income, profits, or estate and gift tax.

¶83 Technical Advice Memoranda

Technical advice memoranda (TAMs) are written determinations containing advice or guidance furnished by the IRS National Office upon request of a District Director or an Appeals Officer in response to any technical or procedural

---

[47] Rev. Proc. 2004-1, IRB 2004-1, 1.
[48] Rev. Proc. 2004-1, IRB 2004-1, 1.

[49] Reg. § 601.201(c)(4).
[50] Rev. Proc. 2004-1, IRB 2004-1, 1.

question that develops during any stage of any proceeding on the interpretation and proper application of tax law, tax treaties, regulations (¶71), revenue rulings (¶74), or other precedents published by the National Office to a specific set of facts (see sample at ¶120).[51] Seeking technical advice from the National Office is discretionary with a District Director. Requests for TAMs generally are given priority and are processed immediately.

District Directors may request technical advice on any technical or procedural question that develops during the audit of a return or claim for refund of a taxpayer. In addition, while the case is under the jurisdiction of the District Director, a taxpayer, or representative, may request that an issue be referred to the National Office for technical advice on the grounds that a lack of uniformity exists as to the disposition of the issue or that the issue is so unusual or complex as to warrant consideration by the National Office. Although a written request by a taxpayer is preferred, an oral request is permitted (¶105).

TAMs must contain the following:

1. A recitation of the pertinent facts having a bearing on the issue;

2. A discussion of the facts, precedents, and reasoning of the National Office; and

3. The conclusions of the National Office.[52]

A revenue procedure explaining when and how the IRS Chief Counsel offices give technical advice to a district director or a chief, appeals office is published annually. It also explains the rights a taxpayer has when a district director or a chief, appeals office, requests technical advice regarding a tax matter.[53]

Only a District Director or Chief, Appeals Office may withdraw a request for technical advice, even a request initiated by the taxpayer. The withdrawal request may be made at any time before the responding transmittal memorandum is signed. However, once the technical advice is issued and is adverse to the taxpayer, the opportunity for further negotiation above the agent level is seriously hampered[54] since both the IRS and the taxpayer are bound by the conclusions of the National Office unless the issue is litigated.

Transmittal memoranda

Where applicable, a notice must accompany a TAM and indicate the intention to disclose the TAM. The notice must include a copy of the version proposed to be open to public inspection and notations of third-party communications, which the District Director or Appeals Office intends to forward to the taxpayer.[55] The reply also must contain a transmittal memorandum. In some cases the transmittal memorandum serves as a vehicle for providing the District

---

[51] Reg. § 601.105(b); Rev. Proc. 2004-2, IRB 2004-1, 83.

[52] Reg. § 601.201(n)(9).

[53] See Rev. Proc. 2004-2, IRB 2004-1, 83.

[54] John W. Bowman, "IRS Procedures: Getting Through the Maze," 158 *Journal of Accountancy* 93, October 1984.

[55] Code Sec. 6110(d) and (f)(1); Rev. Proc. 2004-2, IRB 2004-1, 83.

Director or Appeals Office with administrative information or other information which, under the nondisclosure statutes, or for other reasons, may not be discussed with the taxpayer.

Reliance

Generally, the force and effect of TAMs are the same as that for private letter rulings (¶81). The IRS maintains that a taxpayer may not rely on a TAM issued to another taxpayer since TAMs state the proper interpretation and application of tax laws with respect to a unique set of facts. As with letter rulings, publication of TAMs invites reliance. Prudent tax advisors naturally and appropriately utilize previously issued TAMs to analyze the probable IRS position in their specific tax transaction. Such an analysis provides taxpayer with economic and practical guidance.

Retroactivity

Except in rare or unusual circumstances, a holding in a TAM that is favorable to the taxpayer will be applied retroactively,[56] subject to IRS discretion under Code Sec. 7805(b) (see ¶71.10). A holding that modifies or revokes a holding in a prior TAM also is applied retroactively, unless the new holding is less favorable to the taxpayer than the earlier one. In such case, the new holding is generally not applied to the period in which the taxpayer relied on the prior holding in situations involving continuing transactions.

If a TAM relates to a continuing action or a series of actions, it ordinarily applies until specifically withdrawn or until the conclusion is modified or revoked by enactment of legislation, ratification of a tax treaty, or issuance of a U.S. Supreme Court decision, regulations (¶71), or a revenue ruling (¶74).

Guidelines for prospective application. If the TAM revokes or modifies a letter ruling or another TAM, its holding is not applied retroactively to the taxpayer to whom or for whom the ruling or TAM was issued, provided that:

1. There has been no misstatement or omission of material facts;
2. The facts at the time of the transaction are not materially different from the facts on which the ruling or memorandum was based;
3. There has been no change in the applicable law;
4. In the case of a ruling, it was originally issued on a prospective or proposed transaction; and
5. The taxpayer directly involved in the ruling or TAM acted in good faith in relying on the ruling or TAM and the retroactive revocation would be to the taxpayer's detriment.

¶84 Opinion Letters

An opinion letter is a written statement issued by the National Office as to the acceptability of the form of a master or prototype pension, profit sharing, or

---

[56] Rev. Proc. 2004-2, IRB 2004-1, 83.

stock bonus plan and any related trust or custodial account under Code Secs. 401 and 501(a).[57]

Reliance

Generally, an individual taxpayer may rely on a favorable opinion letter with respect to the form, but not necessarily the substance, of the proposed master or prototype plan. Although an opinion letter is merely advisory, and therefore not binding, it is likely that the IRS would abide by its determination in a pre-plan opinion letter assuming that all material facts are disclosed.

Retroactivity

Retroactive application is not an issue since the opinion letter applies only to a prospective transaction.

¶85 Information Letters

An information letter is a statement issued either by the National Office or by a District Director that calls attention to a well-established interpretation or principle of tax law, without applying it to a specific set of facts.[58] It may be issued if the request indicates that the taxpayer is seeking general information or where the IRS thinks that the general information may help an individual or organization.

Reliance

Information letters are advisory only and, therefore, the IRS is not bound by any statements contained therein. Reliance on information letters for tax planning is discouraged by the IRS.

Retroactivity

Retroactivity is not an issue with respect to information letters because they are published only to impart general information. Since the IRS is not bound by any statements contained in information letters, revocation or modification would automatically be retroactive.

¶86 Technical Memoranda

Technical Memoranda (TMs) are issued by the IRS to summarize and explain published IRS regulations (¶71) (see sample at ¶120). Among other things, TMs state the issues involved, identify controversial legal or policy questions, discuss the reasons for the approach taken by the individuals drafting the regulations, and provide other background information.

Reliance

Generally, the force and effect of TMs are the same as that for private letter rulings (¶81). The use of TMs has declined because new regulations now contain a detailed explanation in their preamble.

---

[57] Reg. § 601.201(a)(4).   [58] Rogovin, "Four R's," 771.

Retroactivity

Generally, retroactivity issues with respect to TMs are the same as those for private letter rulings (¶81).

¶87 Outgoing Treasury Letters

An outgoing Treasury letter is the IRS's response to an incoming Treasury letter submitted by an individual or organization (see sample at ¶120).

Reliance

Outgoing Treasury letters are advisory only and do not bind the IRS to any statements contained therein.

Retroactivity

Retroactivity is not an issue with respect to outgoing Treasury letters because they are published only to impart general information. Since the IRS is not bound by any statements contained in outgoing Treasury letters, revocation or modification is automatically retroactive.

¶88 Closing Agreements

A closing agreement is an agreement between the IRS and a taxpayer on specific issues of liability.[59] Generally, closing agreements are entered into on the basis of the holding of a letter ruling (¶81-83). In appropriate cases, a taxpayer may be asked to enter into a closing agreement as a condition to the issuing of a ruling.[60] If there are more than 25 taxpayers involved and the issue and holding are identical for all taxpayers, a mass closing agreement is entered into with the taxpayer who is authorized by the others to represent the entire group.

It has been held that closing agreements constitute return information and can not be disclosed.[61] The JCT staff recommended that closing agreements of tax-exempt entities should be disclosed in order to assist in the public oversight of such organizations, but did not recommend that closing agreements of taxable entities should be disclosed. Its view was that such agreements are negotiated, and may not represent the IRS view of the law. Further, because such agreements may be fact specific and may not contain all relevant information, they may be misleading if relied upon by others.[62]

Reliance

Closing agreements are binding on the taxpayer and IRS. Unless fraud, malfeasance, or misrepresentation of a material fact can be shown, closing agreements are final as to the particular taxpayer involved.

---

[59] Code Sec. 7121.

[60] See, for example, Rev. Proc. 78-15, 1978-2 CB 488, and Rev. Proc. 85-44, 1985-2 CB 505.

[61] *Tax Analysts*, 99-1 USTC ¶50,345, 53 F.Supp. 2d 449.

[62] Joint Committee on Taxation, Study of Present-Law Taxpayer Confidentiality and Disclosure Provisions as Required by Section 3802 of the Internal Revenue Service Restructuring And Reform Act of 1998, (Vol. II) at 85 n.186.

Retroactivity

Since closing agreements represent a meeting of the minds to resolve a pending tax matter, retroactivity is not an issue. Retroactive application is applicable only to the extent of terms and conditions of the closing agreement.

¶89 Pre-filing Agreements

In 2000, the IRS initiated a pilot program under which large business taxpayers that had a Coordinated Examination Team on site may request a pre-filing agreement (PFA) to resolve specific issues relating to tax returns that they would file later that year.[63] A PFA is a closing agreement under Code Sec. 7121 that specifies the treatment of transactions on a tax return to be filed after the date of the agreement. The PFA program provides a cooperative environment in which taxpayers and the IRS can resolve issues that are likely to be disputed in post-filing examinations and, thus, minimize controversies during examinations. A PFA may also resolve related specific items affecting other tax periods.[64] The IRS later decided to offer the PFA Program on a permanent and expanded basis to Large and Mid-Size Business (LMSB) taxpayers.[65]

The PFA will resolve only the factual characterization of the items at issue, and are not intended to interpret the law. Examples of PFA issues include valuation of assets and the allocation of purchase or sales price among assets acquired or sold; in-house research expenses; and valuation of inventories. Several issues, including advance pricing agreements, employee plans, sham transactions, and partnership items, are excluded from the program.

PFAs are closing agreements entered into pursuant to Code Sec. 7121, the only distinction being that the audit is conducted and completed prior to filing the taxpayer's return. As such, it is the position of the IRS that both PFAs and the information generated or received by the IRS during the PFA process constitute confidential return information as defined by Code Sec. 6103(b)(2)(A), that PFAs are not written determinations under Code Sec. 6110, and, accordingly, are exempt from disclosure to the public under the Freedom of Information Act (FOIA).[66]

Reliance

PFAs are treated as closing agreements, and, therefore, are binding on the taxpayer and IRS. Unless fraud, malfeasance, or misrepresentation of a material fact can be shown, closing agreements are final as to the particular taxpayer involved.

---

[63] Notice 2000-12, IR 2000-7.

[64] See Rev. Proc. 68-16, 1968-1 C.B. 770, which describes the preparation of closing agreements under Code Sec. 7121.

[65] Rev. Proc. 2001-22 , 2001-1 C.B. 745.

[66] Treasury Office of Tax Policy Report to Congress on the Scope and Use of Taxpayer Confidentiality and Disclosure Provisions, Volume I: Study of General Provisions

Retroactivity

Since PFAs represent a meeting of the minds to resolve only factual characterization of items at issue, retroactivity is not an issue. Retroactive application is applicable only to the extent of terms and conditions of the PFA.

¶90 Technical Expedited Advice

Technical expedited advice is technical advice issued in an expedited manner (a TEAM). Subject to agreement among the taxpayer, field or area office, field counsel, and the Associate office, any issue eligible for a TAM can be submitted for TEAM treatment. A TEAM has several characteristics that are different from a TAM, including the following: taxpayer participation in the mandatory presubmission conference, (except for the two situations where taxpayer concurrence is not required for the TEAM procedures); in the event of a tentatively adverse conclusion to the taxpayer or the field, a conference of right will be offered to the taxpayer and the field; and once the conference of right is held, no further conferences will be offered. The procedures associated with the issuance of a TEAM help expedite certain aspects of the TAM process and eliminate some of the requirements that may delay or frustrate the TAM process.

TEAMs help IRS personnel close cases and also help establish and maintain consistent technical positions throughout the IRS. TEAMs are issued only on closed transactions and do not address hypothetical situations. A director or an appeals area director may raise an issue in any tax period, even though a TEAM may have been requested and furnished for the same or similar issue for another tax period.

Reliance

A taxpayer may not rely on a TEAM issued for another taxpayer.

Retroactivity

Except in rare or unusual circumstances, a holding in a TAM or a TEAM that is favorable to the taxpayer is applied retroactively. Moreover, because a TEAM is issued only on a closed transaction, a holding that is adverse to the taxpayer is also applied retroactively, unless the Associate Chief Counsel with jurisdiction over the TEAM exercises the discretionary authority to limit the retroactive effect of the holding.[67]

---

[67] Rev. Proc. 2004-2, IRB 2004-1, 83.

Chapter 10
Pre-decisional and Final Opinions

¶91 Overview

Historically, the IRS had resisted disclosure of various internal memoranda not prepared for public use. However, as the result of court decisions[1] and Congressional mandate in the form of Code Sec. 6110, documents such as General Counsel Memoranda (¶92), Actions on Decisions (¶93), Chief Counsel Advice (¶96), Field Service Advice (¶97) and other intra-agency memoranda (¶98) must be disclosed. Although the IRS now discloses many internal documents, it maintains the position that a taxpayer may not rely on such documents as precedent.

¶92 General Counsel Memoranda

General Counsel Memoranda (GCMs), which are legal analyses prepared by the Office of the Chief Counsel (¶35) (see sample at ¶120).[2] GCMs can not be used or cited as precedent, and are usually written in response to a formal request for legal advice in connection with some revenue rulings (¶74), private letter rulings (¶81), or technical advice memoranda (¶83). GCMs set forth the issue being examined, a brief factual summary, and often a lengthy analysis of the issue and the recommendations and opinions of the Office of the Chief Counsel (¶35).[3]

¶93 Actions on Decisions

It is the policy of the IRS to announce at an early date whether it will follow the holdings in certain cases. An Action on Decision (AOD) is the document making such an announcement. An Action on Decision is issued at the discretion of the IRS only on unappealed issues, decided adverse to the government. Generally, an AOD is issued where guidance would be helpful to IRS personnel working with the same or similar issues. Unlike a Treasury Regulation or a Revenue Ruling, an AOD is not an affirmative statement of IRS position. It is not intended to serve as public guidance and may not be cited as precedent.

An AOD may be relied upon within the IRS only as the conclusion, applying the law to the facts in the particular case at the time the AOD was issued. Caution should be exercised in extending the recommendation of the AOD to similar cases where the facts are different. Moreover, the recommendation in the AOD may be superseded by new legislation, regulations, rulings, cases, or AODs.[4]

---

[1] *Tax Analysts*, 99-1 USTC ¶50,345, 53 F.Supp. 2d 449 and *Taxation With Representation Fund*, DC D of C, 81-1 USTC ¶9252, 646 F2d 666.

[2] GCMs have not been issued since 1995.

[3] Gerald G. Portney, "Letter Rulings: An Endangered Species?," 36 *Tax Lawyer* 757, No. 3, Spring 1983.

[4] Internal Revenue Manual section 4.10.7.2.9.8.1.

Prior to 1991, the IRS published acquiescence or nonacquiescence only in certain regular Tax Court opinions. The IRS expanded its acquiescence program to include other civil tax cases where guidance is determined to be helpful. Accordingly, the IRS may acquiesce or nonacquiese in the holdings of memorandum Tax Court opinions, as well as those of the United States District Courts, Claims Court, and Circuit Courts of Appeal. Regardless of the court deciding the case, the recommendation of any AOD will be published in the Internal Revenue Bulletin.

The recommendation in every AOD is summarized as acquiescence, in result only, or nonacquiescence. Both "acquiescence" and "acquiescence in result only" mean that the IRS accepts the holding of the court in a case and that the IRS will follow it in disposing of cases with the same controlling facts. The following differences are noted:

(a) Acquiescence indicates neither approval nor disapproval of the reasons assigned by the court for its conclusions.

(b) Acquiescence in result only indicates disagreement or concern with some or all of those reasons.

(c) Nonacquiescence signifies that, although no further review was sought, the IRS does not agree with the holding of the court and generally, will not follow the decision in disposing of cases involving other taxpayers. In reference to an opinion of a circuit court of appeals, a nonacquiescence indicates that the IRS will not follow the holding on a nationwide basis. However, the IRS will recognize the precedential impact of the opinion on cases arising within the venue of the deciding circuit.

¶94 Industry Specialization Program Papers

The IRS initiated the Industry Specialization Program (ISP) to promote better identification and development of issues to be covered by its personnel in examining tax returns and to ensure uniform and consistent treatment of issues throughout the examination period. Since its inception, the program has been expanded to include international issues and issues involving employee plans and exempt organizations. The ISP involves ISP Coordinated Issue Papers, Decoordinated Issue Papers, Settlement Guidelines, Industry Specialists, a National Industry Coordinator, Industrywide Studies, Designated Industries, and Identified Industry Cases.[5]

ISP coordinated issue papers are intended to ensure that key industry issues are raised in all cases on a consistent basis and are subsequently resolved using the guidance provided. The papers reflect IRS thinking with respect to key industry compliance issues. They are intended primarily as an audit tool and are designed to be used by revenue agents examining any tax return. The guidance given by them is based on facts known to date and can subsequently change.

---

[5] IRS Handbook 4.4, Industry Specialization Program Handbook.

Reliance

An ISP coordinated issue paper is not treated as an official IRS position. Although ISP Papers are reviewed by the Chief Counsel to determine whether or not they are technically correct, they clearly do not have the status of revenue rulings (¶74) or regulations (¶71). The papers also are not official pronouncements within the meaning of the Internal Revenue Code, and, therefore, there is no statutory authority for taxpayer reliance. One of the justifications for the original decision to issue ISP papers was that, by keeping the papers informal and minimizing the level of review, timely advice could be provided to revenue agents. Some ISP papers may eventually become revenue rulings, but the majority of the papers do not have ruling counterparts. Accordingly, taxpayers may not rely on the papers. Taxpayers seeking protection for a position based on an ISP paper should request a private letter ruling (¶81).

Disclosure

The IRS has made the ISP papers (see sample at ¶120) available to the public and revenue agents will provide a copy of relevant papers to taxpayers in the course of an examination. Additionally, the IRS has determined that the papers may be obtained under FOIA (¶61).

¶95 Market Segment Specialization Program

The Market Segment Specialization Program (MSSP) is an examination program designed to conduct an in-depth, internal study of a particular market segment and using that knowledge to develop guidelines specific to the business environment. A market segment generally consists of an industry, such as construction or entertainment, or a profession, such as attorneys or real estate agents. On rare occasion, an issue requiring specialized auditing techniques, such as passive activity losses or alternative minimum tax, may comprise a market segment. After the MSSP team completes its research and development of methods of operation and completes its case examination processes, it will compare its notes and information, discuss the issue and write an audit technique guide to be used by examiners in future audits.[6]

Reliance

Each audit technique guide carries the warning that under no circumstances should it be used or cited as authority for setting or sustaining a technical position.

Disclosure

By releasing the audit technique guides, the IRS hopes to increase voluntary compliance among taxpayers by educating them in advance. Audit technique guides are to emphasize applicable audit techniques and are not intended to provide lengthy, detailed legal analysis, or resolve controversial or unusual legal issues. Legal issues likely to arise during the audit of the market segment are

---

[6] IRS Handbook 4.3.7, Market Segment Specialization Program (MSSP) Handbook.

identified and summarized, or referenced to the appropriate authority for an analysis of the IRS position. Although the number of audit technique guides released has been limited, the IRS plans to release external versions of its audit technique guides for each of approximately 80 market segments included under the program.

¶96 Chief Counsel Advice

Chief Counsel Advice documents were added to the category of written determinations subject to the public inspection.[7] Chief Counsel Advice is written advice or instruction prepared and issued by any national office component of the Office of Chief Counsel to field employees of the IRS or the Office of Chief Counsel. This advice conveys certain legal interpretations or positions of the IRS or the Office of Chief Counsel concerning existing or former revenue provisions. For these purposes, the term "revenue provisions" includes: the Internal Revenue Code; regulations, revenue rulings, revenue procedures, or other administrative interpretations or guidance, whether published or unpublished (including, for example, other Chief Counsel Advice); tax treaties; and court decisions and opinions.[8]

Chief Counsel Advice includes field service advice, technical assistance to the field, IRS center advice, litigation guideline memoranda, tax litigation bulletins, general litigation bulletins, and criminal tax bulletins. Also included is any document created subsequent to the inclusion of Chief Counsel Advice as written determinations that satisfies the general statutory definition, regardless of their name or designation; and includes any advice or instruction even if the organizations currently issuing them are reorganized or reconstituted as part of any IRS restructuring.[9]

Chief Counsel Advice does not include written recordations of informal telephonic advice by the National Office of Chief Counsel to field personnel of either the IRS or the Office of Chief Counsel. Drafts of Chief Counsel Advice sent to the field for review, criticism, or comment prior to approval within the National Office also need not be made public.

Chief Counsel Advice documents are redacted prior to their public release in a manner similar to that provided for private letter rulings, technical advice memoranda, and determination letters. Specific taxpayers or groups of specific taxpayers who are the subject of Chief Counsel Advice will be afforded the opportunity to participate in the process of redacting the Chief Counsel Advice prior to their public release. Any Chief Counsel Advice that is available for public inspection must also be available by computer telecommunications within one year after issuance.[10]

---

[7] Code Sec. 6110(b)(1).

[8] Conference Committee Report to Tax Relief Extension Act of 1999 (P.L. 106-170).

[9] Act Sec. 3509(d)(3) of P.L. 105-206

[10] Act Sec. 3509(d)(4) of P.L. 105-206

The public inspection of Chief Counsel Advice is to be accomplished only pursuant to the rules and procedures set forth in Code Sec. 6110, and not under those of any other provision of law, such as the FOIA.

Reliance

As with other written determinations, Chief Counsel Advice may not be used or cited as precedent, except as otherwise established by regulation.[11]

Retroactivity

Retroactivity is not an issue since Chief Counsel Advice documents do not represent a final determination of the IRS's position.

¶97 Field Service Advice

Field Service Advice (FSA) are issued by the Office of Chief Counsel in response to requests from field personnel of the Office of Chief Counsel or of the IRS, such as field attorneys, revenue agents and appeals officers. FSA are usually requested for legal guidance with respect to the situation of a specific taxpayer. Although the Office of Chief Counsel has distributed summaries of some FSA, the IRS has argued that FSA are protected from disclosure under the Freedom of Information Act (FOIA). The U.S. Court of Appeals for the D.C. Circuit concluded that no blanket exemption from FOIA disclosure applies to FSA.[12] However, FSA meet the definition of "written determination" for purposes of Code Sec. 6110(a), and therefore are open to public inspection. Code Sec. 6110 is the exclusive means by which to obtain General Counsel Advice, including FSA and TAMs, for public inspection.

Two new types of memorandum have been created, Strategic Advice Memorandum and Background Advice Memorandum. It is likely that these new memoranda will entirely replace field service advice.

Strategic Advice Memorandum

If the field attorney and Associate Chief Counsel office agree that formal advice is needed, the field attorney will prepare a memorandum setting forth the issues upon which advice is being sought, together with a discussion of the facts, law, and conclusions or course of action proposed by the field attorney. The Associate Chief Counsel Office will respond in a strategic advice memorandum (SAM). The SAM will be limited to a discussion of nonroutine factual development, an evaluation of the strengths and weaknesses of the case, and an analysis of the hazards regarding the IRS's technical position. Only the most pertinent facts and legal principles as are necessary to understand the advice will be included. A SAM is essentially a case-development memorandum without the discussion of law or the IRS's legal position. As such, a SAM generally is not required to be published under Code Sec. 6110.

---

[11] Conference Committee Report to Tax Relief Extension Act of 1999 (P.L. 106-170).

[12] *Tax Analysts,* 97-2 USTC ¶ 50,529

Background Advice Memorandum

In a small number of cases, a background advice memorandum (BAM) will be prepared. It will contain a discussion of the law and the IRS's position and include only those facts necessary to adequately describe the transaction or issue upon which advice is being rendered. In contrast to a SAM, a BAM will be more general and provide a legal description of the issue. Accordingly, BAMs are to be published in accordance with Code Sec. 6110. A BAM may be provided in lieu of, or in addition to, a SAM.

Reliance

According to the IRS, field service advice is intended solely to assist a field office in resolving the matter that is the subject of the advice. It does not represent a final determination of the IRS's position, even with respect to the case in which it is requested

Retroactivity

Retroactivity is not an issue since FSA do not represent a final determination of the IRS's position.

¶98 LMSB Directives

The purpose of Large and Mid-Size Business Division (LMSB) Directives is to provide guidelines and instructions to examiners on procedures and administrative aspects of compliance activities to ensure consistent treatment of taxpayers. LMSB Directives are drafted by Industry/Issue teams and are signed by the appropriate LMSB executive.

Industry/Issue teams collaborate with affected internal stakeholders during the drafting stage. Input from external stakeholders may be requested as deemed necessary. The responsible Division management direct the Industry/Issue teams in preparing the directive. Area Counsel provide ongoing review.

Industry Directors, and the Directors, Field Specialists, and International may issue LMSB Directives on Industry specific issues and issues impacting Field Specialists and International Examiners, respectively. The LMSB Commissioner or Commissioner's designee issues LMSB Directives on cross-Industry issues. The Directors will work with the Office of Division Counsel (LMSB) in preparing LMSB Directives.

Directives will be issued on significant and emerging issues and may address: examination planning, issue development, audit techniques, operational guidance, and resource allocation.

LMSB Directives will generally be made available to examiners, specialists, and to the public and will be reviewed annually by the originating office.

Reliance

The directives do not establish IRS position on legal issues and are not legal guidance.

¶98

Retroactivity

Retroactivity is not an issue since the directives do not represent a final determination of the IRS's position.

¶99 Other Intra-and Inter-Agency Memoranda

There are numerous other intra- and inter-agency memoranda available from the IRS. These documents are mentioned here for reference only.

Key documents include Attorney General Opinions, Executive Orders, Treasury Department Orders, routine written communications between IRS personnel, and legal opinions of staff attorneys.

Appeals Settlement Guidelines

Appeals develops settlement guidelines when an issue is coordinated by Compliance. Once the Appeals senior management approves the settlement guidelines, the appeals officer must get the review and concurrence of the Appeals Industry Specialization Program (ISP) coordinator before finalizing a settlement with the taxpayer. Links to file copies are already provided for many issues. In some of these cases, IRS Counsel has recommended that discussion of the hazards of litigation be redacted from these files. Any redactions are so indicated in the individual settlement guideline.

Attorney General Opinions

Inter-agency memoranda may include Attorney General Opinions (AGOs) prepared by the Justice Department at the request of the IRS. IRS reliance on an AGO in formulating its interpretation of a statute is not binding on the Tax Court in its construction of the law.[13]

Legal Advice Issued by Field Attorneys

Documents prepared by Field attorneys in the Office of Chief Counsel that are reviewed by an Associate Office, and subsequently issued to field or service center campus employees of the IRS. It is important to note that such items cannot be used or cited as precedent.

Executive Orders

Inter-agency memoranda may include Executive Orders (EOs) prepared by the Office of the President of the United States.

Treasury Department Orders or Proclamations

Inter-agency memoranda may include Treasury Department Orders (TDOs) or Treasury Department Proclamations prepared by the Treasury Secretary (¶32). TDOs may be used to delegate authority.

Intra-agency Memoranda

Intra-agency memoranda includes written communications between IRS personnel ranging from routine correspondence to recommendations for implementing tax laws.

Legal Opinions of Staff Attorneys

Intra-agency memoranda includes legal opinions of staff attorneys which may be protected under the traditional attorney work-product rules.

---

[13] *Birkin*, 5 BTA 402, Dec. 1885.

Information Letters

An information letter provides general statements of well-defined law without applying them to a specific set of facts.

Chief Counsel Advice Training Materials

CPE Text

Continuing Professional Education (CPE) text is intended for training purposes within the IRS, but gives practitioners insight into the IRS's views on current technical and compliance issues. For example, in August 2000, the IRS released "Exempt Organizations Technical Instruction Program for FY 2001."

Chief Counsel Bulletins

Chief Counsel Bulletins are published periodically by different functions within the Office of Chief Counsel to highlight recent developments in the law. (These documents do not contain proprietary (Official Use Only) information.)

- *Collection, Bankruptcy, and Summonses (CBS) Bulletins.* Published each month, the Collection, Bankruptcy, and Summonses (CBS) Bulletin (previously titled the General Litigation Bulletin) contains summaries of recent court cases of interest to anyone handling general litigation issues, plus summaries of Chief Counsel Advice issued by CBS and available for public inspection under Code Sec. 6110.

- *Criminal Tax Bulletins.* Criminal Tax Bulletins are compilations of recent cases pertaining to criminal tax matters as published by the Office of the Division Counsel/Associate Chief Counsel (Criminal Tax).

- *Disclosure Litigation Bulletins.* Disclosure Litigation Bulletins are published periodically by the Office of the Assistant Chief Counsel (Disclosure & Privacy Law), providing litigation developments and discussion of other disclosure-related issues that arise primarily under Code Sec. 6103, the Freedom of Information Act , and the Privacy Act of 1974 , as these issues relate to IRS and Chief Counsel operations.

Chapter 11
Taxpayer Assistance

¶100 Overview

To assist taxpayers, individuals, corporations, partnerships, and other legal entities to be in compliance with requirements of the Internal Revenue Code and regulations, the IRS develops and issues various forms, instructions, pamphlets, and handbooks.

IRS Publications (¶101) address a variety of general and special topics of concern to taxpayers. Similarly, forms and instructions (¶102) are designed to lead taxpayers step by step through data needed to accurately report information required by law.

The IRS also issues numerous news releases (¶103), pamphlets, and handbooks (¶104) designed to enhance taxpayer advice and guidance. Finally, IRS employees provide taxpayer assistance through direct contact (¶105). While these communication tools are not intended to cover every possible tax situation or to replace the law or change its meaning, they are essential. It is difficult to imagine fair, nondiscriminatory tax administration without this level of tax compliance assistance.

The Office of the National Taxpayer Advocate may issue a taxpayer assistance order if it is determined that the taxpayer is suffering hardship resulting from actions or inactions of the IRS (¶106).

¶101 IRS Publications

IRS Publications (see sample at ¶120) are designed to assist taxpayers, individuals, small business corporations, and other legal entities, who prepare their own income tax returns. Therefore, the tax law is explained in "plain language" so that it will be easier to understand by the average taxpayer. IRS Publications also are issued to explain more complex tax laws that affect individuals, corporations, and partnerships.

A typical IRS Publication highlights changes in the tax law, explains its purpose, defines terminology, lists exemptions, provides several examples, and includes sample worksheets and filled-in forms. Many IRS Publications are updated annually while other are updated as needed.

Some examples of IRS Publications are:

Pub. 1   Your Rights as a Taxpayer
Pub. 17   Your Federal Income Tax
Pub. 54   Tax Guide for U.S. Citizens and Resident Aliens Abroad
Pub. 225   Farmer's Tax Guide
Pub. 334   Tax Guide for Small Businesses

Pub. 463   Travel, Entertainment, Gift, and Car Expenses
Pub. 502   Medical and Dental Expenses

Reliance

Every IRS Publication contains a warning against taxpayer reliance. The IRS warns that information provided covers only the most common tax situations, not every situation, and is not intended to replace the law or change its meaning. Taxpayers also are warned that a particular IRS Publication might cover some subjects on which a court may have made a decision more favorable to them than the IRS interpretation, and that the position taken in the IRS Publication will continue to present the interpretation of the IRS until such differences are resolved by higher court decisions. Thus, taxpayers who choose to follow an interpretation differing from that of the IRS are at risk and must litigate to resolve a disputed tax issue.

IRS Publications do not bind the IRS, but rather act simply as guides. Even so, information provided in IRS Publications provides essential guidance for tax law compliance, particularly in technical or specialized areas. Since IRS Publications provide interpretative guidance at the very lowest level of tax administration, preparation of income tax returns, they are strong indicators, subject to drafting errors or revised interpretations, of the IRS's current position concerning a tax issue.

Retroactivity

Generally, even if a taxpayer has correctly relied on information contained in an IRS Publication at the time of filing his or her income tax return, the IRS may apply a revenue ruling (¶74) retroactively.[1] Similarly, attempts to require the IRS to correct or modify information contained in IRS Publications that may be misleading have been unsuccessful. Although IRS Publications may be confusing, the courts have refused to require corrections where the IRS has published clarifying notices which are disseminated by tax law reporting services.[2]

¶102 Forms and Instructions

The IRS issues forms and instructions for use by taxpayers, individuals, corporations, partnerships, and other legal entities, in complying with the tax laws (see sample at ¶120). The purpose of IRS forms and instructions is to explain the requirements of the Internal Revenue Code (¶22) and regulations (¶71).[3] Many of the forms and instructions are designed to facilitate voluntary compliance with tax law reporting requirements and payment of taxes. Others simply lead taxpayers step-by-step through data needed to accurately report information required by law.[4]

---

[1] *Manocchio*, 78 TC 989, CCH Dec. 39,097, *aff'd*, CA-9, 83-2 USTC ¶9478, 710 F2d 1400; *Koop*, 47 TCM 1107, TC Memo. 1984-75, CCH Dec. 40,998(M); *Kendel*, 50 TCM 1279, TC Memo. 1985-527, CCH Dec. 42,434(M); *Allen*, 51 TC 427, TC Memo. 1986-55, CCH Dec. 42,865(M).

[2] *Resource Technical Consultants (U.S.A.), Inc.*, DC N.Y., 88-1 USTC ¶9111.
[3] Reg. § 601.602(a).
[4] Reg. § 601.602(b).

¶102

The IRS Restructuring and Reform Act of 1998 required the IRS to provide all forms, instructions and publications electronically on the Internet in a searchable database (see ¶54).[5]

Quasi-letter ruling devices

Forms also operate as quasi-letter ruling devices. Appropriate forms may be used as offers in compromise, to make an election, or seek approval of corporate master and prototype pension, profit sharing, or stock bonus plans.

Offers in compromise

The IRS Commissioner may compromise any civil or criminal case arising under the Internal Revenue Code or regulations prior to reference to the Department of Justice for prosecution or defense.[6] An offer in compromise of taxes, interest, delinquency penalties, or specific penalties may be based on either inability to pay or doubt as to liability. Temporary Regulations, generally effective from July 21, 1999, through July 19, 2002, permit offers in compromise to also be based on economic hardship and exceptional circumstances.[7] Although the IRS may compromise a criminal liability involving the regulatory provisions of the Internal Revenue Code and related statutes, it will not do so if the violations are deliberate and with intent to defraud.

Offers in compromise must be submitted by the taxpayer on Form 656, properly executed, and, if the offer is based on inability to pay, a financial statement must also be submitted on Form 433A, Collection Information Statement for Individuals, or Form 433B, Collection Information Statement for Businesses.[8] There must be strict compliance with the law in order to effect a valid, binding compromise.

An IRS decision to accept a taxpayer's offer in compromise of a tax dispute is subject to disclosure. For a period of one year, a copy of the appropriate Form 7249, Offer Acceptance Report, for each accepted offer will be made available for public inspection in the office of the district director having jurisdiction over the place where the taxpayer resides.[9]

Elections

The Internal Revenue Code and regulations often provide for the taxpayer's election of numerous options, such as accounting method, depreciation method, exclusion from partnership treatment, change of tax year, and so forth, by indicating such an election on a specified form. Some elections are automatic and others require IRS approval. Also, some elections are binding in the year elected, some are irrevocable, some are revocable only with IRS consent, and some may not be revoked by amended return.

---

[5] Act Sec. 2003(d) P.L.105-206.

[6] Code Sec. 7122; Reg. § 601.203(a).

[7] Temporary Reg. § 301.7122-1T(b)(4).

[8] Reg. § 601.203(b); Rev. Proc. 96-38, 1996-2 CB 300.

[9] Code Sec. 6103(k)(1), Internal Revenue Manual Handbook 5.8 section 8.7.

Master or prototype pension plans

Upon request, the IRS will furnish a written opinion as to the acceptability of the form of any master or prototype pension plan designed to include groups of self-employed individuals who may adopt the plan.[10] There are three types of previously approved pension plans of self-employed individuals for which the IRS provides forms for submission: master plan; prototype plan; and variable form plan.

A master plan is a form of plan in which the funding organization, trust, custodial account, or insurer, is specified in the sponsor's application, and a prototype plan is a form of plan in which the funding organization is specified in the adopting employer's application. A variable form plan is either a master or prototype plan that permits an employer to select various options relating to such basic provisions as employee coverage, contributions, benefits, and vesting.

A favorable determination letter as to the qualification of a pension or profit sharing plan and the exempt status of any related trust or custodial account is not required. Finally, since a determination (¶82) as to the qualification of a particular employer's plan can be made only with regard to facts peculiar to such employer, a letter expressing the opinion (¶84) of the IRS as to the acceptability of the form of a master or prototype plan does not constitute a ruling or determination as to the qualification of a plan as adopted by any individual employer or as to the exempt status of a related trust or custodial account.

Reliance

Generally, forms and instructions do not bind the IRS and are not intended to replace the law or change its meaning. Rather, they are prepared by the IRS to assist taxpayers in compliance with the law by providing them with step-by-step instructions to guide them in the application of the law to their particular circumstances. Therefore, taxpayers who rely solely on IRS forms and instructions are at risk.

However, forms may have the force and effect of law if prepared pursuant to statutory direction. See, for example, the special rules for allocation of the Generation-Skipping Transfer exemption under Code Sec. 2632(a)(2).

Retroactivity

Since forms and instructions are provided for guidance only, retroactive application is not an issue.

¶103 Technical Information Releases and News Releases

Technical Information Releases (TIRs) allow the IRS to expeditiously disseminate information to the technical press and tax specialists concerning important fast-breaking technical developments. News releases are issued by the IRS and Treasury Department to representatives of major news media to announce items of general, topical rather than technical interest (see sample at ¶120).

---

[10] Reg. § 601.201(p).

¶103

Reliance

Because TIRs and news releases merely announce items of general interest rather than provide interpretations of the tax laws, there is no reliance issue. For example, where news releases announce new revenue rulings (¶74) or revenue procedures (¶75), reliance may be based on the primary documents.

Retroactivity

Since news releases are generally for information and guidance only, retroactive application is not an issue.

¶104 Pamphlets and Handbooks

Pamphlets and handbooks, including those that are part of the Internal Revenue Manual, are published by the IRS to provide taxpayer information or instruction ranging from advice to guidance. Such publications are intended to disseminate information required to facilitate uniform compliance with tax laws and fair administration of the federal tax system.

Handbooks

Handbooks are manuals or references that provide information or instruction on a particular subject. The IRS issues and maintains numerous handbooks such as the following:

1. Disclosure of Official Information Handbook;
2. Problem Resolution Program Handbook;
3. Delinquent Return Refund Hold Program Handbook;
4. Appeals Manual;
5. Audit Technique Handbook;
6. Internal Management Document System Handbook;
7. Partnership Control System Handbook;
8. Natural Disaster and Emergency Relief Handbook;
9. Taxpayer Advocate Program Handbook;
10. Penalty Handbook;
11. Managers Security Handbook;
12. Automated Underreporter Managers and Coordinators Handbook;
13. AIMS/Processing Handbook;
14. Fraud Handbook;
15. Statute of Limitations Handbook; and
16. Employment Tax Handbook.

Pamphlets

Pamphlets, on the other hand, are short publications with a paper cover and no binding. Pamphlets provide general taxpayer information and are often disseminated through the public library system. An example of a pamphlet is the

"Freedom of Information Reading Room" brochure which provides the location, hours, purpose, and a brief description of documents available for public inspection and copying (¶66).

Reliance

Generally, pamphlets and handbooks act as guides that merely state the IRS's current understanding of the regulations (¶71) and, thus, do not bind the IRS. In fact, one federal appellate court has held that such government publications do not bind the IRS regardless of the promises they contain.[11]

However, where a pamphlet specifically promises that the IRS will follow the rules and procedures set forth in the pamphlet until such time as the rules might be modified in regulations (¶71) or IRS publications (¶101) and that any such modification that might be adverse to a taxpayer would be applied prospectively only, two other federal appellate courts have deemed it an abuse of discretion to apply such a modifying regulation retroactively.[12]

Retroactivity

The appropriate test for determining whether retroactivity is an abuse of discretion is:

1. Whether the taxpayer had justifiably relied on settled law that is altered by the regulations; and

2. Whether the retroactive application of the regulations would create "an inordinately harsh result."[13]

The Tax Court, agreeing with this position in denying retroactivity of a new final regulation where the taxpayers had relied on a statement in an IRS handbook indicating that any modifications would be applied prospectively only, concluded that, when sections of the Internal Revenue Code are designed to induce taxpayers to follow a course of behavior for which they have no other motives, the IRS cannot, in fairness, complain when the desired compliance is forthcoming and the taxpayers take the IRS Commissioner (¶34) at his word.[14]

The Tax Court found an abuse of discretion even though an existing proposed regulation was counter to information provided in the IRS handbook and final regulations (¶71) were promulgated and effective five days before the taxpayer took action in reliance on information provided in the handbook. According to the Tax Court, the taxpayers who followed the guidelines in the handbook were merely adhering to the most reliable information available.

¶105 Oral Communications

Oral communications may result from statements made by agents during the audit process, for example, when taxpayers, individuals, corporations, part-

---

[11] *CWT Farms, Inc.*, CA-11, 85-1 USTC ¶9277, 755 F2d 790, aff'g 79 TC 1054, CCH Dec. 39,583.

[12] *Gehl Co.*, CA-7, 86-2 USTC ¶9530, 795 F2d 1324; *LeCroy Research Systems Corp.*, CA-2, 85-1 USTC ¶9107, 751 F2d 123, rev'g on other grounds, 47 TCM 1345, TC Memo. 1984-145, CCH Dec. 41,086(M).

[13] *Gehl Co.*, CA-7, 86-2 USTC ¶9530, 795 F2d 1324, 1332.

[14] *Addison International, Inc.*, 90 TC 1207, No. 78, CCH Dec. 44,840 aff'd CA-6, 89-2 USTC ¶9573, 887 F2d 660.

nerships, or other legal entities request assistance or information regarding determination letters (¶82). The IRS even provides a toll-free number for answering federal tax questions to help taxpayers file their returns.

Private rulings and determinations

The IRS does not issue private letter rulings (¶81) or determination letters (¶82) upon oral requests.[15] IRS officials and employees ordinarily will not discuss a substantive tax issue with a taxpayer or his representative prior to the receipt of a request for a ruling.[16]

Technical assistance

However, a taxpayer may seek oral technical assistance in the preparation of his or her return or report, pursuant to established procedures. Such oral advice is advisory only, and the IRS is not bound to recognize it in the examination of the taxpayer's return.

Agents' interpretations of the law

Similarly, the IRS is not bound by the erroneous interpretation of the law by one of its agents.[17] Generally, as with private letter rulings (¶81) or determination letters (¶82), such oral communications are informal opinion or advisory only. However, as with all general rules there are exceptions. The courts have held that the taxpayer should be permitted to prohibit the IRS from denying or changing its position in cases where:

1. There has been a waiver of sovereign immunity both as to liability and as to suit;

2. The agent whose conduct is relied upon to work as an estoppel acted within the scope of his authority lawfully conferred; and

3. Application of the doctrine would not bring a result that is either inequitable or contrary to law.[18]

Reliance

Generally, oral opinions and advice of IRS personnel are not binding on the IRS. The IRS routinely advises taxpayers who seek assistance that it is not liable for incorrect answers or errors. The taxpayer is also advised that he or she is still responsible for payment of the correct tax and, thus, any penalties that may result from substantial underpayments of the correct tax.

Retroactivity

Since oral communications are generally not binding on the IRS and are provided for advice and guidance only, retroactive application is not an issue.

---

[15] Reg. § 601.201(k).

[16] Rev. Proc 2004-1, IRB 2004-1, 1.

[17] *Burk,* 51 TCM 1156, TC Memo. 1986-233, CCH Dec. 43,099(M); *Norden-Ketay Corp.,* CA-2, 63-2 USTC ¶9575, 319 F2d 902 (cert. denied 375 US 953); *Binder,* CA-9, 39-2 USTC ¶9789, 107 F2d 812.

[18] Rogovin, "Four R's," 775 and footnote 107; *Smale & Robinson, Inc. v. U.S.,* DC Calif., 54-2 USTC ¶9539, 123 FSupp 457; *Interstate Fire Ins. Co. v. U.S.,* DC Tenn., 63-1 USTC ¶9358, 215 FSupp 586.

¶106 Taxpayer Assistance Orders

Upon application filed by a taxpayer or the taxpayer's duly authorized representative with the Office of the National Taxpayer Advocate (formerly with the Office of Ombudsman), the National Taxpayer Advocate (formerly the ombudsman) may issue a taxpayer assistance order (TAO) if he or she determines that the taxpayer is suffering or is about to suffer a significant hardship as a result of the manner in which the internal revenue laws are being administered by the IRS, or if the taxpayer meets other requirements as prescribed by regulation.[19] Generally, the taxpayer will apply for a TAO by filing Form 911 (Application for Taxpayer Assistance Order to Relieve Hardship) with the IRS Problem Resolution Office in the district where the taxpayer resides. In lieu of Form 911 the taxpayer may file a written statement that contains the required information.[20]

The National Taxpayer Advocate has broad authority to take any action permitted by law with respect to taxpayers who would otherwise suffer a significant hardship as a result of the manner in which the IRS is administering the tax laws.[21]

Significant hardship is a subjective determination and is to be made on a case-by-case basis. In an effort to make the determination of significant hardship less subjective, the IRS Restructuring and Reform Act of 1998 (P.L. 105-206) amended Code Sec. 7811(a) to include a list of four circumstances that constitute significant hardship: (1) there is an immediate threat of adverse action; (2) there has been a delay of more than 30 days in resolving the taxpayer's account problems; (3) the taxpayer will have to incur significant costs (including fees for professional services) if relief is not granted; or (4) the taxpayer will suffer irreparable injury, or a long-term adverse impact, if relief is not granted. This is not an exhaustive list of what constitutes significant hardship; a TAO may also be issued in other circumstances where the National Taxpayer Advocate determines that the taxpayer is or will suffer significant hardship. In addition, Code Sec. 7811(a)(3), as amended, directs the National Taxpayer Advocate to construe all of the applicable factors in whatever manner is most favorable to the taxpayer whenever he/she determines that any IRS employee involved in the case is not following applicable published administrative guidance, including the Internal Revenue Manual.

The terms of a taxpayer assistance order may require the Secretary of the Treasury to release any property of the taxpayer that was subject to levy. Also, the order can require the Secretary to cease any action, take any action as permitted by law, or refrain from taking any action, with respect to the taxpayer, regarding collections, bankruptcies and receiverships, discoveries of liabilities and enforcements of title, or any other provision of law that is specifically described by the National Taxpayer Advocate in the order. The National Tax-

---

[19] Code Sec. 7811(a)(1).
[20] See Reg. §301.7811-1(b)(1).

[21] Code Sec. 7811(b)(2).

payer Advocate can specify a time period within which the action required in the taxpayer assistance order must be completed.

A taxpayer assistance order may be modified or rescinded only by the National Taxpayer Advocate, the Commissioner of Internal Revenue or the Deputy Commissioner of Internal Revenue and only if a written explanation of the reasons for modification or rescission is provided to the National Taxpayer Advocate.[22] The National Taxpayer Advocate may issue a taxpayer assistance order and take any of the actions described above in the absence of an application by the taxpayer.[23]

Reliance

The IRS is required to follow the terms of a TAO.

Retroactivity

A TAO can require the IRS to cease an action, take an action or refrain from taking an action.

---

[22] Code Sec. 7811(c).   [23] Code Sec. 7811(e).

Chapter 12
Summary

¶110 IRS Positions

The IRS routinely publishes official rulings and procedures to promote correct and uniform application of the tax laws by IRS personnel and to assist taxpayers in attaining maximum voluntary compliance.

Regulations, revenue rulings, and revenue procedures

Regulations (proposed, temporary, and final) (¶¶71-73), revenue rulings (¶74), and revenue procedures (¶75) must be published in the *Federal Register* (¶51) and also are published in the Internal Revenue Bulletin (¶52) and disseminated to the public by private tax services.

Announcements and notices (¶79) that contain guidance of a substantive or procedural nature and are used when guidance is needed quickly also have taken on added significance equal to that of a revenue ruling or revenue procedure when designated by the IRS as an "administrative pronouncement."

Advance rulings and determinations

In addition, the IRS administers a letter ruling program (¶80) designed to disclose a variety of advance written rulings and determinations, including private letter rulings (¶81), determination letters (¶82), and technical advice memoranda (¶83). This program provides taxpayers and IRS personnel with guidance as to a position that the IRS will likely take with regards to a contemplated transaction.

Internal memoranda

In response to the Freedom of Information Act (¶61), the Privacy Act (¶63), the Electronic Freedom of Information Act (¶67) and other laws relating to IRS disclosure, the IRS discloses many internal memoranda to the public. The Taxpayer Bill of Rights and Taxpayer Bill of Rights 2 also provide taxpayers several additional rights in dealing with the IRS that will have an important impact on taxpayer/IRS interaction and the disclosure of internal memoranda and procedures (¶64).

Among these documents are general counsel memoranda (¶92), actions on decisions (¶93), technical memoranda (¶86), Chief Counsel Advice(¶96) and Field Service Advice (¶97).

Taxpayer information and guidance

Numerous other documents are issued by the IRS to provide taxpayer guidance and assistance and enhance voluntary compliance with the tax laws. Some of these documents, such as forms and instructions (¶102) and IRS Publications (¶101), are specifically designed to assist individuals in compiling and reporting data necessary to determine and remit tax payments. Others, such as pamphlets and handbooks (¶104), technical information releases (¶103), and general news releases (¶103), are used to clarify IRS positions and disseminate information of general interest. The Office of the National Taxpayer Advocate may issue a taxpayer assistance order it is determined that the taxpayer is suffering hardship resulting from actions or inactions of the IRS (¶106).

¶111 Reliance

The degree of reliance that taxpayers may place on an IRS position depends on the type of position and its purpose. Taxpayer reliance is affected by the authority of the IRS Commissioner (¶34) to modify or revoke regulations and rulings.

Regulations

Regulations (¶71) and Treasury Decisions (¶71) on matters of administration, procedure or exercising a discretion conferred by statute have the force and effect of law and are binding upon taxpayers to the same extent as the statute itself. Temporary regulations (¶72) are considered to be adopted regulations and may be relied on by taxpayers to the same extent as final regulations. However, proposed regulations (¶73) may not be relied on by taxpayers to support a tax position.

Revenue rulings and revenue procedures

Although revenue rulings (¶74) and revenue procedures (¶75) do not have the force and effect of regulations, they are published to provide precedents to be used in the disposition of other cases and may be cited and relied upon for that purpose. Notices and announcements made public on or after December 28, 1987 (¶79), containing substantive or procedural guidance, and so designated by the IRS, can be relied on by taxpayers to the same extent that they may rely on revenue rulings and revenue procedures.

Advance rulings and determinations

Congress specifically determined that, unless the IRS provides otherwise, advance, written rulings and determinations such as private letter rulings (¶81), determination letters (¶82), and technical advice memoranda (¶83), may not be used or cited as precedent. However, many courts, though conceding that such documents have no precedential force, have given weight to such advance rulings.

Internal memoranda

It is the stated policy of the IRS to publish as much of the internal management documents, such as the Internal Revenue Manual (¶76), Commissioner Delegation Orders (¶77), and Chief Counsel orders and notices (¶78), as is necessary for understanding of revenue procedures. Such documents are directive and not mandatory and, therefore, taxpayers have no vested right to the benefit of the procedures when the IRS deviates from its own internal rules.

However, although these procedures are not binding, they provide insight into the inner-workings of the IRS.

Although there is no statutory language indicating that general counsel memoranda (¶92) and actions on decisions (¶93) cannot be used as precedent, the IRS contends that such documents are nothing more than internal memoranda that underlie actions and, thus, are not elevated to the status of official agency documents. While such information may provide valuable insights into the IRS's decision making process, taxpayers assume the risk of reliance.

Taxpayer information and guidance

Taxpayers who rely on information provided in IRS publications (¶101), forms and instructions (¶102), or pamphlets and handbooks (¶104), also assume the risk of reliance. These publications are designed to assist taxpayers by leading them step-by-step through the voluntary tax compliance and tax return preparation process.

Generally, oral opinions and advice of IRS personnel are also not binding on the IRS. Exceptions include properly executed offers in compromise (¶102) and certain elections made by filing appropriate tax forms (¶102).

The courts disagree with respect to reliance on information published in IRS handbooks.

Dissemination of information concerning important technical developments or announcements of items of general interest present no reliance issue. Where news releases (¶103) announce new revenue rulings or revenue procedures, reliance may be based on the primary documents. However, taxpayers may rely on certain technical information releases where the announcements are ministerial in nature.

¶112 Retroactivity

Whether the IRS Commissioner modifies or revokes IRS positions retroactively or prospectively only is of key importance. There is a presumption of retroactive application. Generally, prospective application is within the discretion of the IRS.

Regulations

There is a general prohibition on retroactive regulations. Generally final regulations are not effective before the earliest of the following: date on which such regulation is filed with the Federal Register, date any proposed or temporary regulation to which the final regulation relates was filed with the Federal Register, or the date on which any notice substantially describing the expected contents of the final regulation is issued to the public (¶71).

Revenue rulings and revenue procedures

A revenue ruling (¶74), other than one relating to the qualification of pension, annuity, profit sharing, stock bonus, and bond purchase plans, applies retroactively, unless it includes a specific statement indicating the extent to which it is to be applied without retroactive effect. However, courts have refused to retroactively apply revenue rulings where the IRS abused its discretion by inconsistent administration of provisions of the applicable revenue ruling or where a taxpayer justifiably relies in good faith upon the IRS's prior revenue ruling.

Revenue procedures (¶75) are generally applied prospectively only. Thus, a taxpayer may rely on a revised revenue procedure where he or she is not informed of the retroactivity of the later revenue procedure.

Advance rulings and determinations

Private letter rulings (¶81), except to the extent incorporated in a closing agreement (¶88), may be revoked or modified at any time under appropriate circumstances. If a ruling is revoked or modified, the revocation or modification applies to all years open under the statutes, unless the IRS exercises its discretion to limit the retroactive effect.

It is IRS policy that, except in rare or unusual circumstances, revocation of a ruling issued to a taxpayer whose tax liability was directly involved will be prospective only, assuming that all material facts have been disclosed.

Except in rare or unusual circumstances, holdings in technical advice memoranda (¶83) that are favorable to taxpayers will be applied retroactively. A holding that modifies or revokes a prior TAM is also applied retroactively, unless the new holding is less favorable to the taxpayer than the earlier one. In such case, where continuing transactions are involved the new holding is generally not applied to the period in which the taxpayer relied on the prior holding.

If the TAM revokes or modifies a letter ruling or another TAM, its holding is not applied retroactively to the taxpayer to whom the TAM was issued, provided that all material facts have been disclosed.

Internal memoranda

Retroactivity is not an issue with respect to internal memoranda (¶91).

Taxpayer information and guidance

Retroactivity is not an issue with respect to IRS documents that are published to provide general or technical information or that provide taxpayer guidance and assistance in voluntary compliance with the tax laws (¶100). Since the IRS is not bound by statements made in such documents, revocation or modification is automatically retroactive.

¶113 The Future of Publication and Disclosure

The history of publication and disclosure of IRS documents has evolved significantly. Demands for advance information interpreting federal tax laws have proliferated as tax planning has emerged as a major industry in the United States. The trend has been to provide more, better and timely advance information to facilitate taxpayers' voluntary compliance with federal tax laws.

¶113

New and modified regulations and rulings must keep pace with rapidly changing, complex tax laws. Since publication invites reliance, taxpayers must be aware of the degree of reliance that may be placed on various publications. The key to reliance is the knowledge that regulations and rulings will not be revoked or modified retroactively to the detriment of taxpayers.

The IRS and private publishers have made great strides in providing the best available information to the public expeditiously. Without this effort, implementation of the recent massive changes to the IRC would have been difficult if not impossible. Continued and growing requirements for disclosure of a variety of documents dictate that the IRS and private publishers must continue to adapt and redouble their efforts to provide timely, accurate information. Many of the documents are now available electronically, and we can expect electronic transmission of tax research materials to further accelerate.

Thorough tax research, planning, and advice is predicated on a basic understanding of the essential elements of tax administration. Uniformity and fairness are keys to a successful tax administration system. Publication and reliability are the conduits.

APPENDICES

¶120 Appendix A—Sample IRS Documents

A sample of key IRS positions, advance rulings, and documents issued for information and guidance appears on the pages listed below.

.01 Notice of Proposed Rulemaking

A general notice of proposed rulemaking (NPR) (¶51) must, with exceptions, be published in the *Federal Register* and must include the following:

1. A statement of the time, place, and nature of public rulemaking proceedings;

2. Reference to the legal authority under which the rule is proposed; and

3. Either the terms or substance of the proposed rule or a description of the subjects and issues involved.

The following is an excerpt of a notice of proposed rulemaking.

Proposed Regulation, Proposed Amendments of Regulations (REG-171386–03), August 5, 2004

AGENCY: Internal Revenue Service (IRS), Treasury.

ACTION: Notice of proposed rulemaking by cross-reference to temporary regulations.

SUMMARY: In the Rules and Regulations section of this issue of the **Federal Register**, the IRS is issuing temporary regulations relating to an election that may be made by noncorporate taxpayers to treat qualified dividend income as investment income for purposes of calculating the deduction for investment interest. The text of those temporary regulations also serves as the text of these proposed regulations.

DATES: Written or electronic comments and requests for a public hearing must be received by November 3, 2004.

ADDRESSES: Send submissions to: CC:PA:LPD:PR (REG-171386-03), room 5203, Internal Revenue Service, POB 7604, Ben Franklin Station, Washington, D.C. 20044. Alternatively, submissions may be hand-delivered Monday through Friday between the hours of 8 a.m. and 4 p.m. to: CC:PA:LPD:PR (REG-171386-03), Courier's Desk, Internal Revenue Service, 1111 Constitution Avenue, N.W., Washington, D.C.

Taxpayers also may submit comments electronically to the IRS internet site at *www.irs.gov/regs* or via the Federal eRulemaking Portal at *www.regulations.gov* (indicate IRS and REG-171386-03 or RIN 1545-BD16).

FOR FURTHER INFORMATION CONTACT: Concerning submission of comments or requesting a hearing, LaNita Van Dyke, (202) 622-7180; concerning the proposed regulations, Amy Pfalzgraf, (202) 622-4950 (not toll-free numbers).

SUPPLEMENTARY INFORMATION:

Background and Explanation of Provisions

Temporary regulations in the Rules and Regulations section of this issue of the Federal Register amend the Income Tax Regulations (26 CFR Part 1) relating to section 163(d)(4)(B) of the Internal Revenue Code. The temporary regulations provide rules regarding the time and manner for making an election under section 163(d)(4)(B) to treat qualified dividend income as investment income for

¶120.01

purposes of calculating the deduction for investment interest. The text of the temporary regulations also serves as the text of these proposed regulations. The preamble to the temporary regulations explains the amendments.

Special Analyses

It has been determined that this notice of proposed rulemaking is not a significant regulatory action as defined in Executive Order 12866. Therefore, a regulatory assessment is not required. It also has been determined that section 553(b) of the Administrative Procedure Act (5 U.S.C. chapter 5) does not apply to these regulations, and because the regulations do not impose a collection of information on small entities, the Regulatory Flexibility Act (5 U.S.C. chapter 6) does not apply. Pursuant to section 7805(f) of the Internal Revenue Code, this notice of proposed rulemaking will be submitted to the Chief Counsel for Advocacy of the Small Business Administration for comment on its impact on small business.

Comments and Requests for a Public Hearing

Before these proposed regulations are adopted as final regulations, consideration will be given to any written comments (a signed original and eight (8) copies) or electronic comments that are submitted timely to the IRS. The IRS and Treasury Department request comments on the clarity of the proposed rules and how they can be made easier to understand. All comments will be available for public inspection and copying. A public hearing will be scheduled if requested in writing by any person that timely submits written comments. If a public hearing is scheduled, notice of the date, time, and place for the public hearing will be published in the **Federal Register.**

Drafting Information

The principal author of these regulations is Amy Pfalzgraf of the Office of Associate Chief Counsel (Income Tax & Accounting). However, other personnel from the IRS and Treasury Department participated in their development.

.02 Regulations

Regulations are authorized by Code Sec. 7805 and explain the IRS's position, prescribe operation rules, and provide the mechanics for compliance with the various federal income tax laws (¶71). The following is a sample Regulation.

§1.141-16 Effective dates for qualified private activity bond provisions.—
(a) *Scope.* The effective dates of this section apply for purposes of §§1.142-0 through 1.142-2, 1.144-0 through 1.144-2, 1.147-0 through 1.147-2, and 1.150-4.

(b) *Effective dates.* Except as otherwise provided in this section, the regulations designated in paragraph (a) of this section apply to bonds issued on or after May 16, 1997, (the effective date).

(c) *Permissive application.* The regulations designated in paragraph (a) of this section may be applied by issuers in whole, but not in part, to bonds outstanding on the effective date. For this purpose, issuers may apply §1.142-2 without

¶120.02

regard to paragraph (c)(3) thereof to failures to properly use proceeds that occur on or after April 21, 2003.

(d) *Certain remedial actions*

(1) *General rule.* The provisions of § 1.142-2(e) apply to failures to properly use proceeds that occur on or after August 13, 2004 and may be applied by issuers to failures to properly use proceeds that occur on or after May 14, 2004, provided that the bonds are subject to § 1.142-2.

(2) *Special rule for allocations of nonqualified bonds.* For purposes of § 1.142-2(e)(2), in addition to the allocation methods permitted in § 1.142-2(e)(2), an issuer may treat bonds with the longest maturities (determined on a bond-by-bond basis) as the nonqualified bonds, but only with respect to failures to properly use proceeds that occur on or after May 14, 2004 with respect to bonds sold before August 13, 2004.

.01 Historical Comment: T.D. 8712 1/10/97. Amended by T.D. 9150 8/12/2004.

.03 Treasury Decisions

When regulations are issued in final, permanent form, they are promulgated by a document called a Treasury Decision (T.D.) (¶71). By way of distinction, the term "regulation" has come to be restricted to the provisions of the organized bodies of regulations and the term "Treasury Decision" to the instructions and interpretations issued by the IRS Commissioner with the approval of the Treasury Secretary. The following is a sample Treasury Decision.

Treasury Decision 9149, August 10, 2004

AGENCY: Internal Revenue Service (IRS), Treasury.

ACTION: Final and temporary regulations.

SUMMARY: This document contains final and temporary regulations relating to the obligations of persons that receive payments for air transportation or communications services subject to excise tax when persons liable for tax refuse to pay the tax. These temporary regulations affect persons that receive payments subject to tax and persons liable for those taxes. The text of the temporary regulations also serves as the text of the proposed regulations (REG-163909-02) set forth in the notice of proposed rulemaking on this subject in the Proposed Rules section in this issue of the **Federal Register**.

DATES: *Effective Date:* These regulations are effective October 1, 2004.

Applicability Date: For dates of applicability, see §§ 40.6302(c)-3T(b)(2)(ii) and 49.4291-1T.

FOR FURTHER INFORMATION CONTACT: Taylor Cortright (202) 622-3130 (not a toll-free number).

SUPPLEMENTARY INFORMATION:

Background

This document contains amendments to the Excise Tax Procedural Regulations (26 CFR part 40) and the Facilities and Services Excise Tax Regulations (26 CFR part 49). Section 4251 of the Internal Revenue Code (Code) imposes an excise tax on amounts paid for certain communications services. Sections 4261(a) and (b) impose excise taxes on amounts paid for taxable transportation of persons by air. Section 4261(e)(3) provides that any amount paid to an air carrier or related party for the right to provide mileage awards for (or other reductions in the cost of) any transportation of persons by air is treated for purposes of section 4261(a) as an amount paid for taxable transportation and is therefore subject to tax. Section 4261(c) imposes an excise tax on any amount paid for the air transportation of persons that begins or ends in the United States. Section 4271 imposes an excise tax on amounts paid for taxable transportation of property by air. These taxes collectively are referred to as collected excise taxes.

For each of the collected excise taxes, the person liable for the tax is the person making the payment on which tax is imposed (the taxpayer). Under section 4291, the person receiving the payment on which tax is imposed (the collector) generally must collect the tax from the person making the payment and pay it over to the government.

If the taxpayer refuses to pay the tax the collector is required, under § 49.4291-1, to report this refusal to the IRS. The IRS will then assert the tax against the taxpayer. Current regulations do not specify the time within which the collector must report this refusal to the IRS.

Collectors are responsible for filing returns with respect to the collected excise taxes and for making deposits of tax as required by section 6302. Section 40.6302(c)-3 provides an alternative method for computing the amount of deposits of collected excise taxes. Under the alternative method, collectors may compute the amount of tax to be deposited on the basis of amounts considered as collected instead of on the basis of actual collections of tax. A person may use the alternative method with respect to a tax only if the person separately accounts for the tax. The separate account must reflect for each month all items of tax that are included in amounts billed or tickets sold to customers during the month and items of adjustment (including bad debts and errors) relating to the tax for prior months within the period of limitations for credits or refunds. When a collector using the alternative method determines that a taxpayer has refused to pay the tax, the collector adjusts the separate account to reflect that the tax was not collected. Current regulations do not specify the time for adjusting the separate account to reflect that refusal.

The temporary regulations provide that the collector must report the refusal to pay the tax to the IRS by the due date of the return on which the tax would have been reported but for the refusal to pay. In addition, the temporary regulations provide that, for a person using the alternative method, the separate account cannot be adjusted to reflect a refusal to pay tax for the month unless such refusal has been reported.

¶120.03

Special Analyses

It has been determined that this Treasury decision is not a significant regulatory action as defined in Executive Order 12866. Therefore, a regulatory assessment is not required. It also has been determined that section 553(b) of the Administrative Procedure Act (5 U.S.C. chapter 5) does not apply to these regulations. For applicability of the the the Regulatory Flexibility Act, please refer to the cross-referenced notice of proposed rulemaking published elsewhere in this issue of the **Federal Register**. Pursuant to section 7805(f) of the Code, these temporary regulations will be submitted to the Chief Counsel for Advocacy of the Small Business Administration for comment on their impact on small business.

Drafting Information

The principal author of these regulations is Patrick S. Kirwan, Office of Associate Chief Counsel (Passthroughs and Special Industries). However, other personnel from the IRS and Treasury Department participated in their development.

* * *

.04 Revenue Rulings

A revenue ruling is an official interpretation by the IRS of the internal revenue laws, related statutes, tax treaties, and regulations that has been published in the Internal Revenue Bulletin (¶52). It is the conclusion of the IRS on how the tax law is applied to an entire set of facts. Revenue rulings are issued only by the IRS National Office and are published for the information and guidance of taxpayers, IRS officials, and other interested parties (¶74). The following is an excerpt of a sample revenue ruling.

Revenue Ruling 2004–80, I.R.B. 2004–32

ISSUE

Is the vehicle described below a truck or a tractor for purposes of the retail excise tax imposed by § 4051 of the Internal Revenue Code?

FACTS

The vehicle tows trailers and semitrailers (trailers); the trailers exceed 35 feet in length and have a gross vehicle weight (GVW) rating of 20,000 pounds. The vehicle has a standard chassis cab (4-door with crew cab), accommodating five passengers, and is outfitted with certain luxury features. The cab has an electric trailer brake control that connects to the brakes of a towed trailer and to a hook up for trailer lights. The vehicle has two storage boxes behind the cab that can accommodate incidental items such as small tools and vehicle repair equipment.

The chassis cab has a GVW rating of 23,000 pounds and a gross combination weight (GCW) rating of 43,000 pounds. The vehicle is equipped with hydraulic disc brakes with a four wheel automatic braking system, a 300 horsepower engine, and a six-speed automatic transmission. The front axle of the vehicle has an 8,000 pound rating and the rear axle has a 15,000 pound rating.

¶120.04

The vehicle has three types of hitching devices: a removable ball gooseneck hitch, a fifth wheel hitch, and a heavy duty trailer receiver hitch. The vehicle's platform, which is approximately 139 inches long, is designed with a rectangular well to accommodate the gooseneck and fifth wheel hitches (bed hitches). This platform slopes at the rear of the rectangular well and has tie-down hooks. Optional removable steel stake rails can be placed around the platform.

LAW AND ANALYSIS

Section 4051(a)(1) imposes an excise tax on the first retail sale of automobile truck chassis and bodies, truck trailer and semitrailer chassis and bodies, and tractors of the kind chiefly used for highway transportation in combination with a trailer or semitrailer. The tax is not limited to commercial vehicles. Thus, a vehicle may be subject to tax even if sold for use or used as a recreational or private tow vehicle rather than for commercial purposes.

Section 145.4051-1(e)(1)(i) of the Temporary Excise Tax Regulations Under the Highway Revenue Act of 1982 (Pub. L. 97-424) defines "tractor" as a highway vehicle primarily designed to tow a vehicle, such as a trailer or semitrailer, but does not carry cargo on the same chassis as the engine. A vehicle equipped with air brakes and/or towing package will be presumed to be primarily designed as a tractor.

Section 145.4051-1(e)(2) defines "truck" as a highway vehicle that is primarily designed to transport its load on the same chassis as the engine even if it is also equipped to tow a vehicle, such as a trailer or semitrailer.

"Primarily" means "principally" or "of first importance." See Malat v. Riddle, 383 U.S. 569 (1966), 1966-1 C.B. 184. "Primarily" does not mean "exclusive." See Rev. Rul. 77-36, 1977-1 C.B. 347. Therefore, in the context of the primarily designed test, the reference in § 145.4051-1(e)(1)(i) to vehicles not carrying cargo on the same chassis as the engine does not require an absolute inability to carry any cargo on the vehicle's chassis. This limitation may be satisfied even if the vehicle can carry incidental items of cargo when towing a trailer or semitrailer or is capable of carrying limited amounts of cargo when not engaged in its primary function of towing a trailer or semitrailer.

Under the primarily designed test, a vehicle that can both carry cargo on its chassis and tow a trailer is characterized as either a truck or tractor depending on which function is of greater importance. The function for which a vehicle is primarily designed is evidenced by physical characteristics such as the vehicle's capacity to tow a vehicle, carry cargo, and operate (including brake) safely when towing or carrying a cargo. Cargo carrying capacity depends on the vehicle's GVW rating and the configuration of the vehicle's bed or platform. Towing capacity depends on the vehicle's GVW and GCW ratings and whether the vehicle is configured to tow a trailer or semitrailer.

* * *

HOLDING

The vehicle is a tractor for purposes of § 4051.

¶ 120.04

DRAFTING INFORMATION

The principal author of this revenue ruling is Celia Gabrysh of the Office of Associate Chief Counsel (Passthroughs and Special Industries). For further information regarding this revenue ruling contact Celia Gabrysh at (202) 622-3130 (not a toll-free call).

* * *

.05 Revenue Procedures

A revenue procedure is an official statement of procedure published in the Internal Revenue Bulletin (¶52) that either affects the rights or duties of taxpayers or other members of the public under the Internal Revenue Code and related statutes and regulations, or, although not necessarily affecting the rights and duties of the public, should be a matter of public knowledge (¶75). The following is a sample revenue procedure.

Revenue Procedure 2004-48, July 19, 2004

SECTION 1. PURPOSE

This revenue procedure provides a simplified method for taxpayers to request relief for a late S corporation election and a late corporate classification election which was intended to be effective on the same date that the S corporation election was intended to be effective. Generally, this revenue procedure provides that certain eligible entities may be granted relief if the entity satisfies the requirements of section 4 of this revenue procedure.

SECTION 2. BACKGROUND

.01 *S Corporation Elections.*

(1) *In general.* Section 1361(a)(1) of the Internal Revenue Code provides that the term "S corporation" means, with respect to any taxable year, a small business corporation for which an election under § 1362(a) is in effect for that year.

Section 1362(b)(1) provides that a corporation may make an election to be treated as an S corporation for any taxable year (A) at any time during the preceding taxable year, or (B) at any time during the taxable year and on or before the 15th day of the 3rd month of the taxable year.

* * *

SECTION 3. SCOPE

.01 *In General.* An eligible entity that seeks to be classified as a subchapter S corporation must elect to be classified as an association under § 301.7701-3(c)(1)(i) by filing Form 8832 and must elect to be an S corporation under § 1362(a) by filing Form 2553, Election by a Small Business Corporation. In many situations, an entity may timely file Form 2553 but fail to file the Form 8832. Section 301.7701-3T(c)(1)(v)(C) applies to these situations and deems an eligible entity that timely files a Form 2553 to also have filed a Form 8832. In other situations, an eligible entity fails to file a timely Form 2553. In these situations,

301.7701-3T(c) (1) (v) (C) does not apply and the entity would be required to obtain relief in a letter ruling. This revenue procedure provides a simplified method for requesting relief for those situations not covered by § 301.7701-3T, provided that the requirements of sections 4.01 and 4.02 of this revenue procedure are satisfied. The method provided in this revenue procedure is in lieu of to the letter ruling process ordinarily used to obtain relief for late elections under §§ 1362(b)(5), 301.9100-1, and 301.9100-3. Accordingly, user fees do not apply to corrective action under this revenue procedure.

.02 *Relief if this Revenue Procedure is not Applicable* An entity that does not meet the requirements for relief or is denied relief under this revenue procedure may seek relief by requesting a letter ruling. The procedural requirements for requesting a letter ruling are described in Rev. Proc. 2004-1, 2004-1 I.R.B. 1., or its successors.

SECTION 4. RELIEF FOR LATE S CORPORATION ELECTION AND LATE CORPORATE CLASSIFICATION ELECTION

.01 *Eligibility for Relief.* An entity may request relief under of this revenue procedure if the following requirements are met:

(1) The entity is an eligible entity as defined in § 301.7701-3(a);

(2) The entity intended to be classified as a corporation as of the intended effective date of the S corporation status;

(3) The entity fails to qualify as a corporation solely because Form 8832 was not timely filed under § 301.7100-3(c)(1)(i), or Form 8832 was not deemed to have been filed under § 301.7701-3T(c)(1)(v)(C);

(4) In addition to section 4.01(3) of this section, the entity fails to qualify as an S corporation on the intended effective date of the S corporation status solely because the S corporation election was not filed timely pursuant to § 1362(b); and

(5) The entity has reasonable cause for its failure to file timely the S corporation election and the entity classification election.

* * *

SECTION 5. EFFECTIVE DATE

This revenue procedure is effective July 20, 2004. Any entity that meets the requirements of this revenue procedure as of July 20, 2004 may seek relief under this revenue procedure. This revenue procedure applies to requests pending with the Service on July 20, 2004.

.06 Internal Revenue Manual

The Internal Revenue Manual (IRM) is a compilation of instructions promulgated by the IRS for the guidance of its employees when administering the income tax laws (¶76). The following is an excerpt from the Internal Revenue Manual.

SECTION 5.8.7.2.2.1, Return for Inadequate Estimated or Insufficient Withholding Tax Payments

Date document last amended: 5-15-2004

1. A processable offer may be returned when the investigation reveals the taxpayer does not have sufficient estimated tax paid or income tax withheld to cover the current year estimated tax due.

EXAMPLE:

While investigating an offer in compromise on July 15, 2004 you learn that the taxpayer has an extension until August 15, 2004 to file their 2003 Form 1040. You must determine whether the taxpayer has sufficient income tax withheld or estimated taxes paid for the entire 2003 tax year as well as for the first two quarters of the 2004 tax year.

The requirement to have adequate estimated tax paid prior to consideration of an offer applies to corporate as well as individual taxpayers.

2. Prior to returning an offer for this reason the following actions must be taken:

- A determination must be made if the taxpayer has earned sufficient taxable income to require estimated payments or income tax withholding for the year(s) in question and a calculation must be made of the amount of tax that should have been paid in estimated tax payments to date (or withheld) on the income earned.

- Contact with the taxpayer or representative must be made explaining the calculated non-compliance. A request for payment of an estimated tax payment must be made to bring the taxpayer current. A reasonable deadline for responding must be given along with a warning that the offer will be returned if the payment is not received by the deadline set.

- All of the above must be clearly documented in the case history on AOIC.

3. A return for failing to make required estimated tax payments or insufficient withheld tax requires approval of a Group Manger in the field or a Unit Manager in COIC.

.07 Litigation Guideline Memo

Litigation Guideline Memoranda provide information and instruction relating to litigating procedures and methods, and standards and criteria on issues and matters of significant interest to litigating attorneys in the Office of Chief Counsel. The following is an excerpt of a litigation guideline memo.

PROSECUTION STANDARDS, CT-1

May 21, 1992

I. BACKGROUND

This is to incorporate Text 131.1 (revised 3-1-88) of the Internal Revenue Service Law Enforcement Manual IX, and applies to all criminal tax cases.

II. OVERVIEW

¶120.07

Text 131.1

(1) Except as provided in (3) and (4) below, the following criteria apply to income tax investigations:

(a) Criminal prosecution will be recommended under IRC 7201 only if the average yearly additional tax for criminal purposes is $2,500 or more in cases which utilize the specific item method of proof and involve uncomplicated fact patterns.

(b) In IRC 7201 cases that utilize an indirect method of proof or involve complex and sophisticated evasion schemes, criminal prosecution will be recommended only if the additional tax for criminal purposes totals at least $10,000 for the prosecution period, and the additional tax for criminal purposes for any single year within that period is at least $3,000. Thus, in a two year case involving an indirect method of proof and/or a complex evasion scheme, the average yearly additional tax for criminal purposes must be larger than in strongly preferred three year cases, in order for the aggregate liability to total $10,000 for the prosecution period.

(c) Criminal prosecution will be recommended under IRC 7203 (in non-community property states) and under IRC 7206(1) only if the evidence indicates that the average yearly additional tax for criminal purposes would be $2,500 or more. In the community property states of Arizona, California, Idaho, Louisiana, Nevada, New Mexico, Texas, Washington, and Wisconsin, criminal prosecution will be recommended under IRC 7203 only if the evidence indicates that the average yearly additional tax for criminal purposes would be $1,500 or more. The evidence supporting the additional tax should be as fully developed as possible.

(d) Criminal prosecution will be recommended in altered-document type cases (IRC 7207) only if the additional tax for criminal purposes is $500 or more for any year in question.

(2) Investigative preference will be given to cases that span three prosecution years rather than cases involving violations provable as to only one or two years. This preference is particularly relevant where an indirect method of proof is utilized to establish the tax offense.

(3) Criminal prosecution may be recommended even though the additional tax for criminal purposes averages less than the dollar amount prescribed in (1) above in cases where flagrant or repetitious conduct is so egregious that resort to the criminal sanctions becomes warranted. For example:

(a) Where the taxpayer has persisted in attempting to mislead the investigating agents or has seriously attempted to conceal his or her fraudulent schemes, e.g., by submitting false documents or attempting to suborn false statements by witnesses;

(b) Where the case involves a scheme known to be in frequent use by other taxpayers, and this widespread use is believed to have an adverse affect on voluntary compliance;

(c) Where the facts and circumstances are so flagrant as to warrant the conclusion that a reasonable probability of conviction exists, thus differentiating the case in a manner clearly distinguishing it from others involving a small additional tax for criminal purposes.

* * *

.08 Commissioner Delegation Orders

Redelegation of authority by the IRS Commissioner is announced by Commissioner Delegation Orders (CDOs) (¶77). The following is a sample Commissioner Delegation Order.

Commissioner's Delegation Order No. DO-4-33, June 16, 2003

Authority to Sign Form 870-IS, Waiver of Collection Restrictions in Innocent Spouse Cases

(1) **Authority:** The authority to sign Form 870-IS, Waiver of Collection Restrictions in Innocent Spouse Cases, on behalf of the Commissioner, for claims filed under Section 6015 of the Internal Revenue Code.

(2) **Delegated to:** W&I Cincinnati Centralized Innocent Spouse Operations Managers; SB/SE Compliance Technical Services Examination Group Managers; Appeals Team Managers.

(3) **Redelegation:** This authority may be not redelegated.

(4) **Source of Authority:** IRC section 6015; Treasury Regulation Sections 1.6015-1 through 1.6015-9, and Treasury Order 150-10.

(5) To the extent that authority previously exercised consistent with the order may require ratification, it is hereby affirmed and ratified.

Signed: Bob Wenzel, Deputy Commissioner Services and Enforcement

.09 Announcements

Announcements issued by the IRS may contain guidance of a substantive or procedural nature and are used when guidance is needed quickly (¶79). The following is a sample Announcement.

IRS Announcement 2004-61, July 19, 2004

The IRS is requesting information from the public on the application of the Code Sec. 4251 communications tax to new communications technologies. Specifically, the IRS is soliciting information on how current technology should be treated within the description of telephonic or telephonic quality communications in the definitions of local and toll telephone service provided in Code Sec. 4252. The IRS may address these issues in future proposed regulations. To ensure that any new regulations accurately reflect the state of technology, the IRS is asking that communications service providers submit comments and suggestions describing the various technologies, services, and methods of transmission currently available for transmitting data and voice communications and how they should be treated under Code Sec. 4251.

Communications services that are subject to the Code Sec. 4251 tax are defined in Code Sec. 4252, which was enacted in its current form in 1965. Code Sec. 4252 defines local and toll telephone service in terms of telephonic or

¶120.08

telephonic quality communications, which means voice quality services. Since 1965, numerous communications services have been developed and marketed, the methods of transmission have expanded, and the industry has been deregulated. Consequently, the applicability of Code Sec. 4251 to certain services has been called into question.

Comments must be received by September 29, 2004, and should be sent to: CC:PA:LPD:PR (REG-137076-02), Room 5203, Internal Revenue Service, POB 7604, Ben Franklin Station, Washington, D.C. 20044. Comments can also be submitted electronically via the IRS web site at www.irs.gov/regs or via the Federal eRulemaking Portal at www.regulations.gov. Electronic comments should note "IRS and REG-137076-02."

.10 Notices

Notices issued by the IRS may contain guidance of a substantive or procedural nature and are used when guidance is needed quickly (¶79). The following is a sample Notice.

Cumulative Bulletin Notice 2004-54, August 16, 2004

I. PURPOSE

This notice provides that the Internal Revenue Service will permit income tax return preparers to sign original returns, amended returns, or requests for filing extensions by rubber stamp, mechanical device, or computer software program.

II. BACKGROUND

Section 6061 of the Internal Revenue Code generally provides that any tax return, statement, or other document shall be signed in accordance with forms or regulations prescribed by the Secretary. Section 6695(b) imposes a monetary penalty on income tax return preparers who fail to sign a return. Treas. Reg. § 1.6695-1T(b) requires an income tax return preparer to sign a return after it is completed and before the return is presented to the taxpayer for signature.

III. REQUIREMENTS FOR USE OF ALTERNATIVE METHODS OF SIGNING

This notice authorizes income tax return preparers to sign original returns, amended returns, and requests for filing extensions by means of a rubber stamp, mechanical device or computer software program. These alternative methods of signing must include either a facsimile of the individual preparer's signature or the individual preparer's printed name. Income tax return preparers utilizing one of these alternative means are personally responsible for affixing their signatures to returns or requests for extension.

Income tax return preparers who use alternative methods of signing must provide all of the other preparer information that is required on returns and extensions, such as the name, address, relevant employer identification number, the preparer's individual identification number (social security number or preparer tax identification number), and phone number.

This notice applies only to income tax return preparers as defined by Treas. Reg. § 301.7701-15(a) and does not alter the signature requirements for any other type of document currently required to be manually signed, such as elections, applications for changes in accounting method, powers of attorney or consent forms. In addition, this notice does not alter the requirement that tax returns or requests for filing extensions be signed by the person (*i.e.*, the taxpayer) making the return or the request by handwritten signature or other authorized means.

IV. EFFECTIVE DATE

This notice applies to any original return, amended return, or request for filing extension filed on or after January 1, 2004.

.11 Private Letter Rulings

A private letter ruling (also referred to as "letter ruling" or "private ruling") is a written response issued to a taxpayer by the National Office that interprets and applies the tax laws to that taxpayer's specific set of facts (¶ 81). The following is an excerpt of a private letter ruling.

Letter Ruling 200433006, April 26, 2004

This is in reference to a Form 1128, Application to Adopt, Change, or Retain a Tax Year, submitted on behalf of the taxpayer requesting permission to change its accounting period, for federal income tax purposes, from a taxable year ending December 31, to a taxable year ending September 30, effective Year 1. The taxpayer has requested that the Form 1128 be considered timely filed under the authority contained in § 301.9100-3 of the Procedure and Administration Regulations.

Based on the facts and information submitted and the representations made, it is held that the taxpayer has acted reasonably and in good faith, and that the granting of relief will not prejudice the interests of the government. Accordingly, the requirements of the regulations for the granting of relief have been satisfied in this case, and the taxpayer's late filed Form 1128 requesting permission to change to a taxable year ending September 30, effective Year 1, is considered timely filed.

Since a change in accounting period under Rev. Proc. 2002-37 is under the jurisdiction of the Director, Internal Revenue Service Center, where the taxpayer's returns are filed, we have forwarded the application to the Director, Ogden Service Center. Any further communication regarding this matter should be directed to the Ogden Service Center.

The ruling contained in this letter is based upon facts and representations submitted by the taxpayer and accompanied by a penalty of perjury statement executed by an appropriate party. This office has not verified any of the material submitted in support of the request for a ruling. Verification of the factual information, representations, and other data may be required as part of an examination process.

This ruling addresses the granting of § 301.9100-3 relief only. No opinion is expressed regarding the tax treatment of the instant transaction under the provi-

¶120.11

sions of any other sections of the Code or regulations that may be applicable thereto, or regarding the tax treatment of any conditions existing at the time of, or effects resulting from, the instant transaction. Specifically, no opinion is expressed as to whether the taxpayer is permitted under the Code and applicable regulations to change to the tax year requested in the subject Form 1128, or whether the change may be effected under Rev. Proc. 2002-37.

This ruling is directed only to the taxpayer that requested it. Section 6110(k)(3) provides that it may not be used or cited as precedent.

A copy of this letter must be attached to any income tax return to which it is relevant. We enclose a copy of the letter for this purpose. Also enclosed is a copy of the letter showing the deletions proposed to be made when it is disclosed under § 6110.

Sincerely, Robert A. Berkovsky, Branch Chief, Office of Associate Chief Counsel (Income Tax & Accounting).

cc: *****

* * *

.12 Technical Advice Memoranda

Technical advice memoranda (TAMs) are written determinations containing advice or guidance furnished by the IRS National Office upon requests of a District Director or an Appeals Officer in response to any technical or procedural question that develops during any stage of any proceeding on the interpretation and proper application of tax law, tax treaties, regulations (¶71), revenue rulings (¶74), or other precedents published by the National Office to a specific set of facts (¶83). The following is an excerpt of a technical advice memorandum.

Technical Advice Memorandum 200429007, May 28, 2004

DATE: May 28, 2004

TO: Jeffrey Johnson, International Technical Advisor, LM:PFT:I

FROM: Elizabeth Beck, Branch Chief, CC:INTL:BR6

This Technical Assistance responds to your memorandum dated March 10, 2004 requesting advice on the reporting requirements under I.R.C. § 6038A and attendant regulations. Technical Advice does not relate to a specific case and is not binding on Examination or Appeals. This advice is not to be used or cited as precedent.

ISSUES

Under each of the four circumstances presented, whether taxpayer's timely-filed Form 5472 (Information Return of a 25% Foreign-Owned U.S. Corporation or a Foreign Corporation Engaged in a U.S. Trade or Business) is "substantially incomplete" within the meaning of Treas. Reg. § 1.6038A-4(a)(1) and, if so, whether the section 6038A(d) monetary penalty for failure to furnish information should be imposed.

CONCLUSIONS

Our analysis of the facts given in each of the described circumstances shows that the Forms 5472 are likely to be "substantially incomplete" within the meaning of Treas. Reg. § 1.6038A-4(a)(1). However, there is insufficient information to determine whether the penalty should be excused under the reasonable cause provisions of section 6038A(d)(3) and Treas. Reg. § 1.6038A-4(b).

FACTS

All of the scenarios assume that taxpayer:

1) Is a reporting corporation as defined in Treas. Reg. § 1.6038A-1(c) and not a "small corporation" as defined in Treas. Reg. § 1.6038A-4(b)(2)(ii);

2) Timely filed Forms 5472 for transaction(s) during its taxable year with its parent, a foreign corporation;

3) Included all information required by Treas. Reg. § 1.6038A-2(b)(1) and (2) on the Forms 5472; and

4) Did not use estimated amounts on its Forms 5472 because the actual amount of each of the reportable transactions was "determinable" as that term is used in Treas. Reg. § 1.6038A-2(b)(3).

Additional facts that are assumed regarding the transactions in each scenario are:

1) The amount of each type of reportable transactions is larger than $50,000;

2) The amounts reported on the Forms 5472 are identical to the amounts reported for U.S. customs purposes;

3) The magnitude of the erroneous transaction is substantial in relation to all other reportable transactions as correctly reported; and

4) The magnitude of the erroneous transaction is substantial in relation to the reporting corporation's volume of business and overall financial situation.

DISCUSSION

Section 6038A—In General

Before addressing each specific question, a general overview of section 6038A and its attendant regulations is appropriate.

In 1987, in order to permit the Internal Revenue Service ("Service") to obtain information necessary to audit transactions between certain foreign-owned U.S. companies ("reporting corporations") and other related parties, Congress enacted section 6038A which expanded various reporting and record-keeping requirements of these reporting corporations. Staff of Joint Committee on Taxation, 99th Cong., 2nd Sess., *General Explanation of the Tax Reform Act of 1986* (JCS-10-87) at 1053-1054 (J.Comm. Print 1987). Later, in 1989, Congress significantly revised section 6038A to provide the Service with additional tools for auditing transactions between foreign-owned U.S. corporations and their non-U.S. parent corporations. Congress believed these changes were necessary because the lack of clear jurisdiction for enforcement of summonses coupled with

¶120.12

inadequate foreign standards for record-keeping and preservation of documents had "substantially interfered" with the Service's ability to effectively audit the foreign-owned U.S. companies. As part of the revisions, reporting, record-keeping and document-preservation requirements were expanded and monetary penalties for non-compliance with these requirements increased from $1,000 to $10,000 per incident. H.R. Rep. No. 101-386, 101st Cong., 1st Sess., at 1296-1297 (1989).

* * *

.13 Technical Memoranda

Technical Memoranda (TMs) are issued by the IRS to summarize and explain published IRS regulations (¶86). Among other things, TMs state the issues involved, identify controversial legal or policy questions, discuss the reasons for the approach taken by the individuals drafting the regulations, and provide other background information. The following is a sample Technical Memorandum.

January 12, 1993

MEMORANDUM FOR: Honorable Alan J. Wilensky, Acting Assistant Secretary (Tax Policy)

FROM: Shirley D. Peterson, Commissioner of the Internal Revenue

SUBJECT: Final regulations regarding the extension of time for making elections

There is transmitted herewith final regulations relating to the extension of time for making elections. The Treasury decision eliminates the special transitional rule of § 301.9100-1(b) of the regulations for all elections except those under section 4980A(f)(5) of the Internal Revenue Code. The special transitional rule set specific time limits for taxpayers to request relief for missed elections under subtitles B, C, D, and F. Eliminating the special transitional rule for all elections except those under section 4980A(f)(5) comports with the new standards for granting relief under § 301.9100-1. See Rev. Proc. 92-85, 1992-42 I.R.B. 32.

The Treasury decision is effective retroactively to April 5, 1991.

There are no reporting or recordkeeping requirements in these regulations.

Attachment

.14 Chief Council Advice

Chief Counsel advice is written advice or instruction prepared by any National Office component of the Office of Chief Counsel that is issued to field or service center employees of the IRS or regional or district employees of the Office of Chief Counsel and conveys: any legal interpretation of a revenue provision; any IRS or Office of Chief Counsel position or policy concerning a revenue provision; or any legal interpretation of state law, foreign law or other federal law relating to the assessment or collection of any liability under a revenue provision. The following is an excerpt of a Chief Council advice.

Chief Counsel Advice 200435001, July 28, 2004

TO: Associate Area Counsel, (Small Business/Self-Employed), CC:SB:7:POR:1

FROM: Acting Chief, Branch 1, Office of Associate Chief Counsel (Income Tax and Accounting), CC:ITA:1

SUBJECT: Oregon Child Care Credit

This Chief Counsel Advice responds to your request for assistance. This advice may not be used or cited as precedent.

We understand that your office is assisting a local IRS office in preparing an information letter to be issued under the provisions of section 2.04 of Rev. Proc. 2004-1, 2004-1 I.R.B. 1, 7. Previously, your office forwarded draft text for our review. We reviewed that text and recommend some revisions. The text in the section below reflects our revisions, and we recommend that it be used for the body of the information letter, with appropriate modifications. For example, the local IRS office will need to insert a closing paragraph with contact information.

Text for Letter

This information letter responds to your inquiry concerning whether contributions made under the Oregon Child Care Tax Credit Program (Or. Rev. Stat. § 657A.700 *et seq.*) qualify for a charitable contribution deduction under § 170 of the Internal Revenue Code. Section 2.04 of Revenue Procedure 2004-1, 2004-1 I.R.B. 1, 7, describes an "information letter" as a statement issued by the Internal Revenue Service that calls attention to a well-established interpretation or principle of tax law without applying it to a specific set of facts. An information letter is advisory only and has no binding effect on the Internal Revenue Service.

To summarize the following discussion, a payment for which a benefit of receiving a state income tax credit may be expected raises serious concerns as to the deductibility of such a payment as a charitable contribution on the contributor's federal income tax return. However, if a charitable contribution deduction under § 170 of the Internal Revenue Code is not allowable for federal income tax purposes, it is possible that an equivalent deduction may be allowable under I.R.C. § 162 or § 164, as a payment of state tax. The Service's national office has been informed of this Oregon credit because it is studying various issues concerning the federal tax treatment of state tax credits and whether such issues should be addressed in official published guidance.

* * *

DISCUSSION

Charitable contribution deduction

Section 170(a)(1) of the Internal Revenue Code provides the general rule that, subject to certain limitations, there shall be allowed as a deduction any charitable contribution (as defined in § 170(c)) payment of which is made within a taxable year. See also section 1.170A-1 of the federal income tax regulations.

Generally, to be deductible as a charitable contribution under I.R.C. § 170, a transfer to a charitable organization or government unit must be a gift. A gift for this purpose is a transfer of money or property without receipt of adequate consideration, made with charitable intent. A transfer is not made with charitable

.16 Service Center Advice

The Office of Chief Counsel provides legal advice to IRS service centers and related IRS functions with respect to their tax administration responsibilities. A service center advice is distributed and published to provide consistent legal advice to all affected IRS functions and Counsel offices on matters raised by the various functions. The following is a sample of a service center advice.

Service Center Advice 200235029, July 28, 2002

MEMORANDUM FOR ELIZABETH S. HENN, DEPUTY AREA COUNSEL (NORTHEAST AND MIDATLANTIC AREA), CC:TEGE:NEMA:BAL

FROM: Michael A. Swim, Acting Assistant Chief Counsel (Exempt Organizations/Employment Tax/Government Entities) Office of Division Counsel/Associate Chief Counsel (Tax Exempt and Government Entities), CC:TEGE:EOEG

SUBJECT: FICA Refund Claims Based Upon the Case of *North Dakota State University v. United States*

ATTENTION: Sandra M. Jefferson

This responds to your request for Significant Service Center Advice dated April 25, 2002, in connection with questions posed by the Philadelphia Service Center concerning how to process refund claims filed by taxpayers based on the decision in North Dakota State University v. United States, 255 F.3d 599 (8th Cir. 2001) [2001-2 USTC 50,485]. In accordance with I.R.C. § 6110(k)(3) , this Significant Service Center Advice should not be cited as precedent.

ISSUE

Whether Service Centers should make refund payments to universities and colleges, or university and college professors, who file claims for refunds of the employer or employee portion of Federal Insurance Contributions Act ("FICA") taxes paid based upon the *North Dakota State University* decision.

CONCLUSION

Service Centers should make refunds of FICA taxes only to taxpayers having claims that concern cases that arise within the jurisdiction of the Eighth Circuit of the United States Court of Appeals and that have the exact facts as the facts in the "North Dakota State University case. Cases having the exact facts are cases involving payments to college or university professors made in exchange for the relinquishment of their tenure rights. All other claims of refund of FICA taxes that cite the *North Dakota State University* decision should be denied. As provided in *North Dakota State University v. United States*, AOD CC-2001-08 (December 31, 2001), we will continue to litigate our position in cases having different facts in cases that are appealable to the Eighth Circuit and in all cases in other circuits.

DISCUSSION

The Eighth Circuit of the United States Court of Appeals is the first circuit court to address the issue of whether early retirement benefits paid to tenured university professors should be considered wages for the purposes of FICA. In the *North Dakota State University* case, the IRS argued that the determination of whether early retirement payments made to tenured faculty members are subject to FICA taxes depends upon whether such payments arise out of the employer-employee relationship and not upon whether the payments are made to employees to relinquish a "contractual and constitutionally-protected right." In *Social Security Board v. Nierotko*, 327 U.S. 358 (1946) [66 SCt 637], the Supreme Court stated that the term "wages" is to be broadly interpreted "to import the breadth of coverage" consistent with the purposes of the Social Security Act. Since no statutory exclusion from "wages exists for early requirement payments made to employees or for payments made to employees for relinquishment of tenure rights, and because the payments in this case arise out of the employer-employee context for services rendered by the tenured faculty members for their employer, these payments should be considered wages subject to FICA taxes. The IRS further argued that the payments should be considered wages subject to FICA because the payments were similar to the amounts employees received in relinquishing their seniority rights acquired as a consequence of past services under Rev. Rul. 75-44 , 1975-1 C.B. 15.

.17 Chief Counsel Notice

Chief Counsel notices are temporary directives used to disseminate policies, procedures, instructions and/or delegations of authority to Chief Counsel employees. The following is an excerpt of a Chief Counsel Notice.

Department of the Treasury	Internal Revenue Service	Office of Chief Counsel	Notice
			[CC-2004-023]

June 04, 2004

| | | | Upon incorporation |
| **Subject:** Expert Witness Procedures | | **Cancel Date:** | into CCDM |

Purpose

This notice reiterates the requirements under T.C. Rule 143(f) that expert witnesses sign the expert witness report submitted to the Tax Court and be available to testify at trial.

Discussion

The purpose of expert testimony is to assist the trier of fact to understand the evidence better or to decide a fact in issue. Fed. R. Evid. 702; *RLC Industries v. Commissioner*, 98 T.C. 457 (1992). Experts in the Tax Court typically present their direct testimony in the form of a written report. Specifically, T. C. Rule 143(f)(1) provides that any party who calls an expert witness must submit a written report prepared by the witness setting forth the witness' qualifications, opinion, the data upon which the opinion is based and detailed reasons for the witness' conclusions. Because the report will generally be received into evidence as the

¶120.17

direct testimony of the expert after it is identified by the expert, the report must satisfy the admissibility standards set forth in the Federal Rules of Evidence. In order to establish admissibility of expert testimony, the proponent need only demonstrate that the expert's opinion satisfies the standards of admissibility specified in Fed. R. Evid. 702 and 703.

An expert's testimony will be excluded for failure to comply with T.C. Rule 143(f)(1) unless the failure is shown to be due to good cause and the failure does not unduly prejudice the opposing party. An example of undue prejudice under T.C. Rule 143(f)(1) occurs when the failure significantly impairs the opposing party's ability to crossexamine the expert.

To the extent portions of an expert witness report consist of out-of-court statements by experts who are not available to testify, such statements may be considered hearsay.

Filing Instructions: Binder _____

NO: Circulate ____ Distribute X to: All Personnel X Attorneys ____

    In: _____

    Other _____

Electronic Filename: *CC-2004-023.pdf* Original signed copy in: *CC:FM:PM:P*

While the testifying expert may attempt to adopt those statements, the fact remains that the non-testifying expert is not available for cross-examination of the direct testimony contained in the report. In addition, simply because an expert adopts the words of a report prepared by another does not establish that the expert is familiar with material matters in the report. The proponent of the report must establish that the words, analysis, and opinions in the report are the expert's own work and a reflection of the expert's own expertise.

The trial judge bears a special gatekeeping obligation to ensure that any and all expert testimony is relevant and reliable. *Kumho Tire Co. v. Carmichael*, 526 U.S. 137, 147 (1999); *Daubert v. Merrill Dow Pharmaceuticals, Inc.*, 509 U.S. 579, 589 (1993). Thus, the admissibility of expert testimony is within the sound discretion of the trial judge. *United States v. Gutman*, 725 F.2d 417, 424 (7th Cir. 1984).

To avoid the possibility that the Tax Court will exclude all or a portion of an expert witness report signed by nontestifying experts, Counsel attorneys must produce as witnesses all of the experts who prepared the report.

If you have a case where expert reports have already been submitted to the court signed by multiple experts and you have not identified as witnesses all of the signing expert witnesses, please contact APJP, Branch 3, for guidance. Any additional questions about the provisions of this Notice should be directed to Julie A. Jebe at (202) 622-7950.

_____/s/_____

DEBORAH A. BUTLER

Associate Chief Counsel

(Procedure and Administration)

.18 Outgoing Treasury Letters

An outgoing Treasury letter is the IRS's response to an incoming Treasury letter submitted by an individual or organization (¶87). This informal guidance system has become increasingly popular due to the backlog of IRS regulations and rulings required to administer massive tax law changes enacted by recent major legislation. The following is an excerpt of an outgoing Treasury letter.

DEPARTMENT OF THE TREASURY INTERNAL REVENUE SERVICE WASHINGTON, D.C. 20224

Dear Sir or Madam:

As you may be aware, in 1996, The Bureau of National Affairs, Inc. ("BNA") brought an action against the Internal Revenue Service seeking the public disclosure of all Advance Pricing Agreements ("APAs") completed as of that time, and subsequently brought two additional actions seeking the APAs completed in the intervening periods (these three actions are now consolidated into a single case). A number of procedural motions have been filed during the past three years concerning discovery, culminating in an order issued by a magistrate judge of the U.S. District Court for the District of Columbia, on October 16, 1998, which called for the submission of all APAs subject to the lawsuit for an inspection by the judge in chambers. The APAs were provided to the court pursuant to that order. On November 25, 1998, BNA filed a motion for summary judgment, and it is now incumbent upon the Service to respond to that motion by January 11, 1999.

Since the inception of the APA program, the Service has been of the view that information received or generated by the Service during the APA process relates directly to the potential tax liability of the taxpayer and, therefore, the APA itself is subject to the confidentiality provisions of section 6103 of the Code. Accordingly, the Service has protected APAs in their entirety from disclosure to unauthorized parties. BNA, however, disagrees that APAs should be withheld as section 6103 information in their entirety and claims that they should be released under the Freedom of Information Act. Alternatively, BNA asserts that APAs are "written determinations" subject to section 6110 of the Code. Under section 6110, APAs would be released to the public, but only after the redaction of names, addresses, and other identifying details of the taxpayer, the taxpayer's trade secrets and other commercial or financial information, as well as information subject to protection under the non-disclosure provisions of our income tax treaties.

After extensive consideration of this matter in light of developments since the lawsuit was initially filed, the Service has concluded, and the Department of Justice has concurred, that APAs are "written determinations" covered by section 6110 and that the government should pursue a judicial resolution of the matter under that section. Assuming the court agrees to a resolution of the case based on section 6110, the redaction process to be applied to APAs would be much like the process currently used for the process currently used for the redaction of private

¶120.18

letter rulings. We have attached for your reference an information sheet (in the form of a "Notice of Intention to Disclose") that is provided to taxpayers who receive private letter rulings from the Service.

The redaction process would apply to both APAs that are negotiated in the future and APAs that have been completed since the program's inception. In either circumstance, the taxpayer would be given an opportunity to participate in the redaction process to help the Service ensure that the taxpayer's confidentiality is protected and that sensitive, confidential or proprietary information is removed before the APA is publicly disclosed.

* * *

.19 Information Letter

An information letter provides general statements of well-defined law without applying them to a specific set of facts. Information letters are furnished by the IRS National Office in response to requests by taxpayers, by congresspersons on behalf of constituents, or congresspersons on their own behalf for general information. Information letters are advisory only and have no binding effect on the IRS. The following is an excerpt of an information letter.

Number: INFO 2004-0116

Release Date: 6/30/04

Number: 1362.00-00

Dear ****:

We are responding to your letter on behalf of the Taxpayer, dated November 6, 2003, requesting a late S election effective March 15, 2001. Although we are unable to respond to the request as submitted, this letter provides useful information relating to the request.

According to the information provided, the Taxpayer intended to elect to be an S corporation from its inception, March 15, 2001, but the election was not filed. Rev. Proc. 97-48 and Rev. Proc. 2003-43 do not apply in the case. To obtain relief, the Taxpayer may request a private letter ruling.

Announcement 97-4 (copy enclosed) provides guidance on seeking relief for late S corporation elections and inadvertent invalid S corporation elections. Generally, to request relief for a late or invalid S corporation election you must request a private letter ruling from the National Office. The procedures for requesting a private letter ruling are set out in Rev. Proc. 2004-1 (copy enclosed). In addition, Rev. Proc. 2003-1 requires taxpayers to submit a user fee along with their ruling request. The standard user fee for a private letter ruling is $6,000. *However*, taxpayers with gross income of *less than $1 million* on their last-filed tax return qualify for a *reduced user fee* in the amount of *$500*. If you are eligible to use the reduced fee provision you must include the statement described in '(B)(1)(b) of Appendix A with your request. Please review Appendix B for a sample format for requesting a private letter ruling.

If you decide to submit a formal request for a private letter ruling, please include the proper user fee (if applying under the reduced fee provisions, send a statement certifying gross income), and refer your request to our office by adding the following to the address:

Attn: CC:PA:T

P.O. Box 7604

Ben Franklin Station

Washington, DC 20044

Direct to: CC:PSI:1

Room 5002

By way of introduction, the IRS has a small business website which provides information and various useful links. Visit this special site at *www.irs.gov/smallbiz*. Additionally, you can order a single, free copy of the Small Business Resource Guide CD-ROM, by calling 1-800-829-3676. The CD-ROM provides critical tax information including forms, instructions, and publications, as well as valuable information from a variety of government agencies, non-profit organizations, and educational institutions.

We hope that the above information proves helpful.

.20 General Counsel Memoranda

General Counsel Memoranda (GCMs) are legal analyses prepared by the Office of the Chief Counsel (¶92). GCMs are usually written in response to a formal request for legal advice in connection with some revenue rulings (¶74), private letter rulings (¶81), or technical advice memoranda (¶83). The following is a sample of a General Counsel Memorandum.

General Council Memorandum 39888, April 18, 1995

This responds to a request that we reconsider GCM 39,686, I-203-87 (Dec. 11, 1987) [IRPO ¶1992], *Section 6661 Penalty in Form 1042 Examinations*. GCM 39,686 concluded that the former §6661 penalty for substantial understatement of income taxes does not apply to a withholding agent's substantial understatement of tax on Form 1042, Annual Withholding Tax Return for U.S. Source Income of Foreign Persons. GCM 39,686 reasoned that §1441 of the Internal Revenue Code is not an income tax on the withholding agent within the meaning of §6661, because the tax is not imposed on the income received by the withholding agent. Further, GCM 39,686 reasoned that the legislative history suggests that Congress did not intend to apply this penalty to understatements on a Form 1042.

This conclusion is inconsistent with the Tax Court's decision on a related issue in *Northern Indiana Public Service v. Commissioner*, 101 T.C. 294 (1993) [CCH Dec. 49,329]. *Northern Indiana Public Service* held that the special 6-year period of limitation for assessment, contained in §6501(e)(1), applies where there is an omission of gross income paid to nonresident aliens that exceeds 25 percent of the amount shown on Form 1042. The Tax Court in *Northern Indiana Public Service* rejected the argument that the application of §6501(e)(1) is restricted to income received by a taxpayer. Further, the Tax Court reasoned that §§ 1441 and 1461, which give rise to a withholding agent's liability, impose income taxes. The withholding tax is imposed by § 1441, and the withholding agent is made directly liable for such tax by § 1461. These Code sections are in subtitle A, and subtitle A imposes income taxes.

The tax imposed by § 1441 is an income tax, and, therefore, comes within the literal language of § 6661. The legislative history of § 6661 does not indicate a specific intention to apply the penalty to Form 1042 nor does it indicate any intention to exclude Form 1042. See S. Rep. No. 97-494 (vol.1) 97th Cong., 2d Sess. 272-273 (1982).

In view of the above, we conclude that the § 6661 penalty for substantial understatement of income taxes applies to Form 1042. The penalty provided in § 6662(b)(2) (effective for returns filed after December 31, 1989) for a substantial understatement of income tax is substantially the same as the penalty provided under former § 6661, with certain modifications. Thus, we conclude that the § 6662(b)(2) penalty would also apply to Form 1042.

Accordingly, GCM 39,686 is hereby revoked.

JODY J. BREWSTER

Assistant Chief Counsel

(Income Tax & Accounting)

By: Rudolf M. Planert

Chief, Branch 4

.21 Actions on Decisions

Actions on Decisions (AODs) are legal memoranda that are prepared whenever the IRS loses an issue in a litigated tax case (¶ 93). AODs set forth the issue that was decided against the IRS, provide a brief discussion of the facts, and outline the reasons why the responsible attorney recommended that the IRS either agree, *i.e.*, acquiescence (¶ 42), or disagree, *i.e.*, nonacquiescence (¶ 42), with the court's decision. AODs are not prepared for every decision unfavorable to the IRS. The following is a sample of an Action on Decision.

Sidney L. Olson and Miriam K. Olson v. Commissioner

January 23, 2004

Issue:

1. Whether the distribution of the stock of a controlled corporation by a distributing corporation to the shareholders of the distributing corporation to prevent the potential union of the distributing corporation from claiming that the distributing and controlled corporations constitute a single employer for labor law purposes qualifies as a valid corporate business purpose under § 1.355-2(b) of the Income Tax Regulations. 0355.04-00, 0316.00-00, 0301.01-00, 301.02-00.

Discussion:

This Revised Action on Decision withdraws the Service's acquiescence in the original Action on Decision issued for this case regarding issue (1) of the original Action on Decision. This Revised Action on Decision does not affect the Service's acquiescence regarding issue (2) of the original Action on Decision.

In *Olson*, the stock of Olson Electronics of Cleveland, Inc. ("Cleveland") was held by four individuals and a corporation, Sidal Corp. ("Sidal"), all of the stock of which was owned by two of the individual shareholders of Cleveland. Olson Electronics of Buffalo, Inc. ("Buffalo") was a wholly owned subsidiary of Cleveland. Cleveland was subject to union activities and although an attempt to unionize Cleveland failed, the union threatened to make another attempt after the twelve-month statutory minimum waiting period. Based on advice of labor counsel, Cleveland distributed the stock of Buffalo to its shareholders (except Sidal) to prevent the union (should it win the potential future election) from claiming that Cleveland and Buffalo constituted a single employer, thereby giving it the right to represent the employees of both Cleveland and Buffalo.

* * *

Following the court's decision, the Service has made significant changes to the business purpose regulations under section 355. Under the current regulations, a distribution is carried out for a valid business purpose if it is motivated, in whole or substantial part, by one or more corporate business purposes. In addition, the current regulations provide that if a corporate business purpose can be achieved through a non-taxable transaction that does not involve the distribution of stock of a controlled corporation and which is neither impractical nor unduly expensive, then the distribution is not carried out for that business purpose. Upon reconsideration of the facts of Olson, at the time of the distribution, it was not clear that the distribution could have achieved the taxpayer's stated business objective or that that objective could not have been achieved through means other than a distribution. Specifically, the court did not analyze the implications of labor law and it was not clear that the distribution could have impeded the union's claim that Cleveland and Buffalo constituted a single employer. Hence, it was not clear that the distribution was motivated by the taxpayer's stated business purpose. Had the court employed the analysis now required by the current regulations, it may not have reached the conclusion that the distribution had a valid business purpose. Accordingly, we withdraw our acquiescence in issue (1) of the original Action on Decision.

Recommendation:

1. Withdraw acquiescence.

.22 Industry Specialization Program Papers

Industry Specialization Program (ISP) coordinated issue papers are examination tools used by revenue agents to apply consistent treatment of issues to taxpayers in designated industry categories (¶94). ISP papers set out an issue within an industry category, the facts that the IRS has gathered in determining its treatment of the issue, and the law and analysis supporting the IRS's treatment of the issue. The following is a sample ISP coordinated issue paper.

LOSSES CLAIMED AND INCOME TO BE REPORTED FROM LEASE IN/ LEASE OUT TRANSACTIONS

Effective Date: October 17, 2003

ISSUES

1. Whether taxpayers entering into Lease In/Lease Out (LILO) transactions are entitled to deduct currently rental expense, and to amortize transaction costs resulting from their participation in the transaction under Internal Revenue Code § 162, or whether taxpayers purchased at most a future interest, as in substance dominion and control over the property remain with the Tax Exempt Entity during the period of the Sublease.

2. Whether taxpayers entering into LILO transactions are entitled to deduct interest expense resulting from their participation in the transaction under Internal Revenue Code § 163, or whether the deductions are disallowed on grounds that no amount is paid for the use or forbearance of money.

3. Alternatively, whether taxpayers entering into LILO transactions should be treated under the substance over form doctrine as having entered into a financing arrangement.

* * *

CONCLUSIONS

1. Taxpayers entering into LILO transactions are not entitled to deduct currently rental expense, or to amortize transaction costs resulting from their participation in the transaction under § 162, because taxpayers purchased a future interest, as in substance dominion and control over the property remain with the Tax Exempt Entity during the period of the Sublease.

2. Taxpayers entering into LILO transactions are not entitled to deduct interest expense resulting from their participation in the transaction under § 163, as no amount is paid for the use or forbearance of money.

3. Alternatively, under the appropriate factual circumstances, taxpayers entering into LILO transactions are not entitled to deduct rental expense resulting from their participation in the transaction because the LILO is a financing arrangement rather than a true lease. Under this alternative, taxpayers would not be treated as having purchased a future interest.

FACTS

1. Overview of a Typical LILO Transaction

LILO transactions occur between a U.S. Taxpayer (commonly known, and referred to herein sometimes as, the Equity Investor), and a Tax Exempt Entity. In these transactions, the Tax Exempt Entity (also known as the Lessor/Sublessee) ostensibly leases the property to the Equity Investor (also known as the Lessee/

Sublessor) via a Headlease. The Equity Investor immediately leases the property back to the Tax Exempt Entity through a Sublease. The Equity Investor commonly acts through a domestic Grantor Trust (the Trust) which executes all the agreements in the transaction as an agent. Because the Trust is ignored for tax purposes, the terms "U.S. Taxpayer", "Equity Investor" and "Trust" are used interchangeably in this paper. The Headlease payment(s) by the Equity Investor is necessary to generate the rental expense deductions (and amortizations) claimed for U.S. Tax purposes.

These transactions generally involve a foreign bank or the foreign branch of a domestic bank (Lender) and an affiliate of Lender (the Payment Undertaking Party/Deposit Taker.) Lender is essential to the LILO transaction as it makes the nonrecourse loan used by the Equity Investor to fund the majority of the prepaid (also known as advance) Headlease rental payments made to the Tax Exempt Entity at the beginning of the transaction. The remaining amount used to make the prepayment is supplied by the Equity Investor from its funds (referred to as Equity Investment). Once the Equity Investor prepays a portion of its rental payments, as permitted by the Headlease, rental expense deductions, which comprise the majority of the tax benefits derived from the transaction, purportedly become available. Moreover, the nonrecourse loan creates the claimed interest expense deductions.

* * *

.23 Market Segment Specialization Program

The Market Segment Specialization Program (MSSP) is an examination program designed to conduct an in-depth, internal study of a particular market segment and using that knowledge to develop guidelines specific to the business environment. After study an audit technique guide to be used by examiners in future audits is produced. The following is an excerpt of an MSSP.

AUDIT TECHNIQUE GUIDE FOR THE WINE INDUSTRY

April 1995

NOTE: The taxpayer names and addresses shown in this publication are hypothetical. They were chosen at random from a list of names of American colleges and universities as shown in Webster's Dictionary or from a list of names of counties in the United States as listed in the United States Government Printing Office Style Manual.

INTRODUCTION

The Sacramento District formed the Wine Industry Study (WIS) as part of the implementation of the Market Segment Specialization Program (MSSP). The wine industry was selected because of its relative uniqueness to, and overall economic impact on that district.

The wine industry, for purposes of the study, was defined as the wine making operations in Northern California. While the study focused on wineries, some vineyard operations were included. The information contained in this

¶120.23

package represents information developed and issues raised during examinations within this industry.

The goals of the study were:

1. To determine the nature and extent of noncompliance within the industry

2. To develop an audit techniques guide for the industry

3. To promote voluntary compliance within the industry through consistent treatment of issues and taxpayer education.

CHAPTER 1—OVERVIEW OF WINERY/VINEYARD OPERATIONS

FARMING

The initial step in the making of wine is growing grapes. Specific varieties of grapes are used in making premium wines, but any grape with sugar content can be fermented. Successful wine grape farming is dependent upon proper soil and climatic conditions. These particular geographic regions (appellations) can be conducive to the quality of a particular varietal or to wine grapes in general.

The first step in the development of a vineyard is land clearing. This may be as simple as plowing under existing vegetation to removal of trees and leveling the dirt. Vineyards planted on hillsides must be terraced. Rocks may need to be removed. Typical water sources include wells, above ground storage (ponds), or some form of irrigation district supply. The water is then delivered through sprinkler or drip systems.

In certain cases, the soil may need to be fumigated (sterilized) prior to planting. Various viral, bacterial, and soil-borne pest problems can be minimized through this process. Fumigation consists of injecting chemicals into the soil and then sealing the vineyard with a plastic cover for a few days. The cost of this process can range from $300 to $600§ per acre, depending on the type of chemicals used and the difficulty in application. In addition to fumigation, the land may need some type of soil conditioning, such as the addition of fertilizers, lime, or minerals, to correct deficiencies in the soil.

* * *

.24 IRS Publications

IRS Publications (Pubs) provide explanations and examples reflecting the IRS's interpretation of tax laws, regulations, and court decisions or statistical information intended only for the internal use of the IRS or reproductions of revenue rulings (¶74) or other official pronouncements (¶79). IRS Pubs (see sample at ¶120) are designed to assist taxpayers, individuals, small business corporations, and other legal entities who prepare their own income tax returns (¶101). The following is an excerpt from an IRS Pub.

¶120.24

Department
of the
Treasury

**Internal
Revenue
Service**

Publication 1544
(Rev. May 2003)
Cat. No. 12696A

Reporting Cash Payments of Over $10,000

(Received in a Trade or Business)

Get forms and other information faster and easier by:

Computer • www.irs.gov or **FTP** • ftp.irs.gov

FAX • 703-368-9694 (from your FAX machine)

Introduction

If, in a 12-month period, you receive more than $10,000 in cash from one buyer as a result of a transaction in your trade or business, you must report it to the Internal Revenue Service (IRS) and the Financial Crimes Enforcement Network (FinCEN) on Form 8300, *Report of Cash Payments Over $10,000 Received in a Trade or Business.*

This publication explains why, when, and where to report these cash payments. It also discusses the substantial penalties for not reporting them.

Some organizations do not have to file Form 8300, including financial institutions who must file FinCEN **Form 104** (formerly Form 4789), *Currency Transaction Report,* and casinos who must file FinCEN **Form 103** (formerly Form 8362), *Currency Transaction Report by Casinos.* They are not discussed in this publication.

This publication explains key issues and terms related to Form 8300. You should also read the instructions attached to the form. They explain what to enter on each line.

Why Report These Payments?

Drug dealers and smugglers often use large cash payments to "launder" money from illegal activities. Laundering means converting "dirty" or illegally-gained money to "clean" money.

The government can often trace this laundered money through the payments you report. Laws passed by Congress require you to report these payments. Your compliance with these laws provides valuable information that can stop those who evade taxes and those who profit from the drug trade and other criminal activities.

The USA PATRIOT Act of 2001 increased the scope of these laws to help trace funds used for terrorism.

Who Must File Form 8300?

Generally, any person in a trade or business who receives more than $10,000 in cash in a single transaction or in related transactions must file Form 8300.

For example, you may have to file Form 8300 if you are a dealer in jewelry, furniture, boats, aircraft, or automobiles; a pawnbroker; an attorney; a real estate broker; an insurance company; or a travel agency. Special rules for clerks of federal or state courts are discussed later under *Bail received by court clerks.*

However, you do not have to file Form 8300 if the transaction is not related to your trade or business. For example, if you own a jewelry store and sell your personal automobile for more than $10,000 in cash, you would not submit a Form 8300 for that transaction.

Transaction defined. A "transaction" occurs when:

- Goods, services, or property are sold.

.25 Forms and Instructions

The IRS routinely issues forms and instructions for use by taxpayers, individuals, corporations, partnerships, and other legal entities in complying with the tax laws (¶102). The following is a sample IRS form with instructions.

Form **W-4S**	**Request for Federal Income Tax Withholding From Sick Pay**	OMB No. 1545-0717
Department of the Treasury Internal Revenue Service	▶ Give this form to the third-party payer of your sick pay.	2004

Type or print your full name		Your social security number

Home address (number and street or rural route)

City or town, state, and ZIP code

Claim or identification number (if any) . . . .

I request income tax withholding from my sick pay payments. I want the following amount to be withheld from each payment. (See **Worksheet** below.) . . . . $

Employee's signature ▶   Date ▶

---------------------------- Cut here and give the top part of this form to the payer. Keep the lower part for your records. ----------------------------

Worksheet (Keep for your records. Do not send to the Internal Revenue Service.)

1	Enter amount of adjusted gross income that you expect in 2004	1
2	**If you plan to itemize deductions** on Schedule A (Form 1040), enter the estimated total of your deductions. For 2004, you may have to reduce your itemized deductions if your income is over $142,700 ($71,350 if married filing separately). See **Pub. 919**, How Do I Adjust My Tax Withholding? for details. Call 1-800-829-3676 or visit the IRS Web Site at **www.irs.gov** to order forms and publications. **If you do not plan to itemize deductions,** enter the standard deduction (see the instructions on page 2 for the standard deduction amount, including additional amounts for age and blindness)	2
3	Subtract line 2 from line 1.	3
4	Exemptions. Multiply $3,100 by the number of personal exemptions. For 2004, your personal exemption(s) amount is reduced if your income is over $142,700 if single, $214,050 if married filing jointly or qualifying widow(er), $107,025 if married filing separately, or $178,350 if head of household. See Pub. 919 for details.	4
5	Subtract line 4 from line 3	5
6	Tax. Figure your tax on line 5 by using the 2004 Tax Rate Schedule X, Y, or Z on page 2. **Do not** use the Tax Table or Tax Rate Schedule X, Y, or Z in the 2003 Form 1040, 1040A, or 1040EZ instructions . . .	6
7	Credits (child tax and higher education credits, credit for child and dependent care expenses, etc.) . . .	7
8	Subtract line 7 from line 6	8
9	Estimated income tax withheld and to be withheld from other sources (including amounts withheld due to a prior Form W-4S) during 2004 or paid with Form 1040-ES.	9
10	Subtract line 9 from line 8	10
11	Enter the number of sick pay payments you expect to receive this year to which this Form W-4S will apply	11
12	Divide line 10 by line 11. Round to the nearest dollar. This is the amount that should be withheld from each sick pay payment. Be sure it meets the requirements for the amount that should be withheld, as explained under **Amount to be withheld** below. If it does, enter this amount on Form W-4S above	12

General Instructions

Purpose of form. Give this form to the **third-party payer** of your sick pay, such as an insurance company, if you want Federal income tax withheld from the payments. You are not required to have Federal income tax withheld from sick pay paid by a third party. However, if you choose to request such withholding, Internal Revenue Code sections 3402(o) and 6109 and their regulations require you to provide the information requested on this form. **Do not** use this form if your employer (or its agent) makes the payments because employers are already required to withhold income tax from sick pay.

Note: *If you receive sick pay under a collective bargaining agreement, see your union representative or employer.*

Definition. Sick pay is a payment that you receive:

1. Under a plan your employer takes part in and

2. In place of wages for any period when you are temporarily absent from work because of sickness or injury.

Amount to be withheld. Enter on this form the amount that you want withheld from each payment. The amount that you enter:

● Must be in whole dollars (for example, $35, not $34.50).

● Must be at least $20 a week.

● Must not reduce the net amount of each sick pay payment that you receive to less than $10.

For payments larger or smaller than a regular full payment of sick pay, the amount withheld will be in the same proportion as your regular withholding from sick pay. For example, if your regular full payment of $100 a week normally has $25 (25%) withheld, then $20 (25%) will be withheld from a partial payment of $80.

Caution: *Generally, you may be subject to a penalty if your tax payments during the year are not at least 90% of the tax shown on your tax return. For exceptions and details, see Pub. 505, Tax Withholding and Estimated Tax. You may pay tax during the year through withholding or estimated tax payments or both. To avoid a penalty, make sure that you have enough tax withheld or make estimated tax payments using Form 1040-ES, Estimated Tax for Individuals. You may estimate your income tax liability by using the worksheet above.*

(continued on back)

For Paperwork Reduction Act Notice, see page 2.   Cat. No. 10226E   Form **W-4S** (2004)

¶120.25

.26 Internal Revenue News Releases

Internal Revenue news releases are issued by the IRS to representatives of major news media to announce items of general, topical rather than technical interest (¶ 103). The following is an excerpt of an Internal Revenue news release.

Internal Revenue News Release IR-2004-110, August 19, 2004

The Internal Revenue Service announced new steps to improve reporting and disclosure by tax-exempt "section 527" political groups.

The new initiative will include contacting section 527 political groups whose filings appear to be incomplete, were filed late, or were amended and are materially different from the original filing. The fact that a group is not contacted at this time does not mean that the group's reports have been accepted as correctly filed.

The initiative's launch is timed in advance of key upcoming filing dates so that correct information is available to the public as intended by Congress.

"This effort will help improve the completeness and accuracy of these important public disclosures," said Steven T. Miller, Commissioner of the IRS Tax-Exempt and Government Entities Division. "Our job is to ensure compliance with the law."

The purpose of section 527 groups is to engage in political activities. Under section 527 of the Internal Revenue Code, as modified in June of 2000 and November 2002, certain political groups must periodically file public disclosure reports with the IRS, rather than the Federal Election Commission. The statute requires these organizations to report their contributions and disbursements so that their support and operations are in the public domain in advance of elections.

There has been rapid growth in the activity of these groups. The IRS has identified concerns about dozens of filings from groups representing a wide variety of political and policy interests.

Martha Sullivan, IRS Director of Exempt Organizations, explained that the new effort is intended to step up enforcement of the reporting rules at a critical period. "The statute is very clear that those tax-exempt political organizations reporting to us must make the required disclosures in a timely, accurate manner," Sullivan said. "The IRS is working to make sure this important information is available this fall and that these groups meet their public reporting responsibilities."

In the initial stage of the program, the IRS will immediately begin contacting a cross-section of groups to request that they explain and correct apparent discrepancies in their existing filings prior to upcoming filing deadlines. These deadlines include September 20 (for monthly filers) or October 15 (for quarterly filers), as well as October 21 for pre-election reports.

An organization that fails to timely report, fails to include all required information about contributions and disbursements, or that reports incorrect information is required to pay 35 percent of the amount related to the failure. There is an exception for reasonable cause.

The filings, as well as information on the filing requirements and upcoming dates, are available on the IRS.gov website at www.irs.gov/polorgs. The IRS launched the revised website in July 2003 to make it easier for political organizations to electronically file required documents with the IRS and improve availability of these documents to the public.

This 527 initiative is consistent with the IRS's renewed emphasis on enforcement of the tax laws. One of the IRS's four key service-wide enforcement priorities is to discourage and deter non-compliance within tax-exempt and government entities and misuse of such entities by third parties for tax avoidance and other unintended purposes.

* * *

.27 Treasury Department News Release

Treasury Department news releases are issued by the Treasury Department to announce items under its administration. These items often involve international tax matters, *e.g.*, treaties. The following is an excerpt of a Treasury Department news release.

Treasury Department News Release JS-1849, August 10, 2004.

Today the Treasury Department and the Internal Revenue Service issued Notice 2004-57, to inform taxpayers that the IRS will continue to collect the communications excise tax as it always has, notwithstanding ongoing and conflicting litigation.

Individuals and businesses paying for taxable communications services are required to pay the tax to their phone company together with their payment for the services. The phone companies then forward the taxes collected from their customers to the United States Treasury. Failure to pay the tax to the phone company may result in the imposition of penalties and interest. Taxpayers who believe, based on the ongoing litigation, that they do not owe the tax can preserve any rights they may have to a refund, without risking penalties and interest, by paying the tax to the phone company and filing a claim for refund with the IRS.

Current regulations require phone companies to report the failure of their customers to pay the telephone excise tax, but the regulations do not provide a date by which the report is due. Proposed and temporary regulations are being issued today that provide that date.

* * *

.28 Acquiescences and Nonacquiescences

Whenever the IRS loses an issue in a litigated Tax Court case, the Commissioner has the option, but not the obligation, to either agree or disagree with the court's decision. Agreement with the court's decision is called "acquiescence," and disagreement is referred to as "nonacquiescence" (¶ 42; see also ¶ 93, Actions on Decisions). The following is a sample announcement of acquiescences and nonacquiescences.

Nonacquiescence Announcement, I.R.B. 2004-32

Actions Relating to Decisions of the Tax Court

It is the policy of the Internal Revenue Service to announce at an early date whether it will follow the holdings in certain cases. An Action on Decision is the document making such an announcement. An Action on Decision will be issued at the discretion of the Service only on unappealed issues decided adverse to the government. Generally, an Action on Decision is issued where its guidance would be helpful to Service personnel working with the same or similar issues. Unlike a Treasury Regulation or a Revenue Ruling, an Action on Decision is not an affirmative statement of Service position. It is not intended to serve as public guidance and may not be cited as precedent.

Actions on Decisions shall be relied upon within the Service only as conclusions applying the law to the facts in the particular case at the time the Action on Decision was issued. Caution should be exercised in extending the recommendation of the Action on Decision to similar cases where the facts are different. Moreover, the recommendation in the Action on Decision may be superseded by new legislation, regulations, rulings, cases, or Actions on Decisions.

Prior to 1991, the Service published acquiescence or nonacquiescence only in certain regular Tax Court opinions. The Service has expanded its acquiescence program to include other civil tax cases where guidance is determined to be helpful. Accordingly, the Service now may acquiesce or nonacquiesce in the holdings of memorandum Tax Court opinions, as well as those of the United States District Courts, Claims Court, and Circuit Courts of Appeal. Regardless of the court deciding the case, the recommendation of any Action on Decision will be published in the Internal Revenue Bulletin.

The recommendation in every Action on Decision will be summarized as acquiescence, acquiescence in result only, or nonacquiescence. Both "acquiescence" and "acquiescence in result only" mean that the Service accepts the holding of the court in a case and that the Service will follow it in disposing of cases with the same controlling facts. However, "acquiescence" indicates neither approval nor disapproval of the reasons assigned by the court for its conclusions; whereas, "acquiescence in result only" indicates disagreement or concern with some or all of those reasons. "Nonacquiescence" signifies that, although no further review was sought, the Service does not agree with the holding of the court and, generally, will not follow the decision in disposing of cases involving other taxpayers. In reference to an opinion of a circuit court of appeals, a "nonacquiescence" indicates that the Service will not follow the holding on a nationwide basis. However, the Service will recognize the precedential impact of the opinion on cases arising within the venue of the deciding circuit.

The Actions on Decisions published in the weekly Internal Revenue Bulletin are consolidated semiannually and appear in the first Bulletin for July and the

Cumulative Bulletin for the first half of the year. A semiannual consolidation also appears in the first Bulletin for the following January and in the Cumulative Bulletin for the last half of the year.

The Commissioner does NOT ACQUIESCE in the following decision:

United States v. Roland Harry Macher (In re Macher),[1] 91 AFTR2d 2003-2654, 2003-2 USTC ¶50,537

(Bankr. W.D. Va.), aff'd 303 B.R. 798 (W.D. Va. 2003)

.29 LMSB Industry Director Guidance

Large and Mid-Size Business Division (LMSB) Directives provide guidelines and instructions to examiners on procedures and administrative aspects of compliance activities to ensure consistent treatment of taxpayers. LMSB Directives are drafted by Industry/Issue teams and are signed by the appropriate LMSB executive. The following is an excerpt of LMSB Industry Director Guidance.

2004ARD 165-1, August 26, 2004

DEPARTMENT OF THE TREASURY

INTERNAL REVENUE SERVICE

WASHINGTON, D.C. 20224

August 20, 2004

MEMORANDUM FOR LARGE AND MID-SIZE BUSINESS DIRECTORS AND MANAGERS

FROM: Bobby E. Scott /s/ Bobby E. Scott Industry Director Natural Resources and Construction

SUBJECT: LMSB Alert - Emerging Issue on Look Back Interest for Construction Industry

This memorandum provides information regarding noncompliance of look-back interest under IRC § 460.

Due to the significance and impact of this issue, Natural Resources and Construction industry has designated this an Emerging Issue and has formed an Emerging Issue Team to develop guidance to assist LMSB personnel in identifying and developing the related issues. The goal of the Team will be to look at the Look Back Interest Issue administratively and determine the need for regulatory changes. More information will be forthcoming as the Emerging Issue Team develops this guidance.

---

[1] Nonacquiescence relating to whether a bankruptcy court has the authority to order the United States to process and consider a debtor's plan of reorganization in accordance with procedures applicable to offers in compromise submitted by taxpayers who are not currently in bankruptcy.

In the year of completion, IRC §460 requires income from certain long-term contracts accounted for under the percentage-of-completion method to be "hypothetically" reallocated among the prior taxable years on the basis of actual instead of estimated contract price and costs. Look-back interest is computed on the "hypothetical" underpayment or overpayment of tax that results from this reallocation of income.

Form 8697, Interest Computation Under the Look-Back Method for Completed Long-Term Contracts, is used to compute and report look-back interest due or to be refunded. For each filing year, the taxpayer will either owe look-back interest or be entitled to a refund as the "net" result of computing look-back interest on one or more prior years. Thus, a current filing year may contain both hypothetical overpayments and underpayments for prior years but the net result determines whether look-back interest is owed by the taxpayer or should be refunded.

The taxpayer will file look-back interest one of two ways depending on whether look-back interest is owed or look-back interest is to be received.

1. Look-back Interest Owed by the Taxpayer. The Form 8697 is attached to and filed with the taxpayer's income tax return, thus part of the Master File account. These forms are processed as integral parts of the return.

2. Look-back Interest Due to the Taxpayer. The Form 8697 is filed separately from the tax return and is treated as a manual refund on the Non-Master File account. The taxpayer files with the Cincinnati campus for BMF or the Philadelphia campus for IMF.

Due to the complexity in tax law along with inconsistent filing procedures, the taxpayers either compute the look-back incorrectly or fail to compute the look-back interest when required. Some of the common errors include:

1. Improperly computing interest from the Net Operating Loss (NOL) carry back year rather than the NOL generating year.

2. Improperly changing the interest rate quarterly rather than keeping it the same for the entire annual period.

3. Improperly computing look-back interest at the entity level of a flow-through entity (1065, 1120S) when it is required to be computed at the owner level.

4. Forms 8697 refunds are improperly attached to the tax return reducing the current year's tax liability. Forms 8697 refunds must be filed separately from the income tax return.

5. The cumulative changes to look-back taxable income and look-back tax liability for each re-determination year are not being properly reported on the Form 8697.

Additional information regarding look-back interest can be found on the LMSB Construction Website *http://lmsb.irs.gov/hq/pftg/construction/index.asp* under the Training, Tools, and Resource Materials section.

Field personnel identifying this issue should contact Jeanne Wierman, LMSB PFTG Construction Technical Advisor, at 843-414-1432.

Cc: Bill Conlon, Director of Reporting Compliance, SB/SE Ronnie L. Desbrow, Area Director, Appeals

.30 Field Office Advice

Legal advice issued by field attorneys are documents prepared by field attorneys in the Office of Chief Counsel that are reviewed by an Associate Office, and subsequently issued to field or service center campus employees of the IRS. Such items cannot be used or cited as precedent. Following is an excerpt of a Field Office Advice.

Number: 20042903F

Release Date: 7/16/04

CC:SB:2:PIT:POSTS 167391-03

EFPeduzzi

date: May 13, 2004

to: Ricky Stiff Headquarters Program Manager, Excise Tax

from: Edward F. Peduzzi, Jr., Associate Area Counsel, Area 2

Office of ISP Counsel for Excise Tax

subject: **Mobile Machinery Exception to Definition of Highway Vehicle**

This memorandum responds to your request for assistance dated September 24, 2003. This memorandum should not be cited as precedent.

ISSUE

What are the guidelines for allowing or denying excise tax claims based on the "mobile machinery exception" [hereinafter MME] in cases that had been placed under 1254 suspense[1] awaiting the outcome of litigation in *Schlumberger Technology Corp. & Subs. v. United States*, 55 Fed. Cl. 203, 2003-1 USTC (CCH) 70,200 (Fed. Cl. 2003) [hereinafter *Schlumberger*]and *Florida Power & Light Co. v. United States*, 56 Fed. Cl. 328; 2003-1 USTC (CCH) 70,208 (Fed. Cl. 2003) [hereinafter *FPL*]?

CONCLUSIONS

Distilled from the discussion below, the following guidelines should be analyzed in any application of the MME:

---

[1] Under IRM sections 4.8.2.4, 4.8.2.10.1, and CCDM section 35.8.10.8, "1254 suspense" is initiated when the determination is made that an issue in nondocketed cases at the examination level is the same as the issue involved in a pending federal court tax case, and that it would be advisable to hold the disposition of the nondocketed cases in abeyance until the court case is concluded in order to establish a uniform basis for the disposition of the nondocketed cases.

¶120.30

I. All three tests enumerated in Treas. Reg. § 48.4041-8(b)(2)(i) and Treas. Reg. § 48.4061(a)-1(d)(2)(i) must be met in order for the MME to be applied to a particular highway vehicle.

* * *

DISCLOSURE STATEMENT

This writing may contain privileged information. Any unauthorized disclosure of this writing may have an adverse effect on privileges, such as the attorney client privilege. If disclosure becomes necessary, please contact this office for our views.

_____/s/_____

EDWARD F. PEDUZZI, JR.

Associate Area Counsel

(Small Business/Self-Employed)

¶121 Appendix B—Precedential Value of IRS Documents

The chart on the following page summarizes key IRS documents with a focus on their precedential value and retroactivity. The column "Precedent" indicates that the document has the full force and effect of law and may be cited as precedent. The column "Evidence" indicates that the courts may afford the documents some weight. The column "Advice & Guidance" indicates that the documents are intended to provide information and assist in tax law compliance only. If both the "Advice & Guidance" and "Evidence" columns are checked, there is some authority for limited use of the documents as evidence.

The "Retroactivity/Prospectivity" column indicates the likelihood that a new or revised document will be applied retroactively or only prospectively. To assist in evaluation this categorization has been further refined as follows:

1. "R presumed" indicates that retroactivity is presumed by law and that new or revised rulings will be automatically applied retroactively unless the IRS specifically states otherwise;

2. "R generally" indicates that new or revised rulings will be applied retroactively unless incorporated into a closing agreement or, with respect to a taxpayer whose tax liability was directly involved, where a taxpayer has detrimentally relied on the ruling. The IRS may, at its sole discretion, limit retroactivity;

3. "R usually" indicates that except in rare or unusual circumstances a holding will be applied retroactively only;

4. "R" only indicates that retroactivity is automatic;

5. "P generally" indicates that except in rare or unusual circumstances new or revised procedures will be applied prospectively only; and

6. "N/A" indicates that retroactivity and prospectivity are not issues.

PRECEDENTIAL VALUE OF IRS DOCUMENTS

Document	Precedent	Evidence	Advice & Guidance	Retroactivity/ Prospectivity
Final Regulations	X			P Generally
Temp. Regulations	X			P Generally
Prop. Regulations		X	X	P Generally
Revenue Rulings	X		X	R presumed
Revenue Procedures	X		X	P generally
Treasury Decisions	X		X	R presumed
Letter Rulings		X	X	R generally
Chief Counsel Advice		X	X	R generally
Field Service Advice		X	X	R generally
TAMs		X	X	R usually
Determinations			X	R usually
TMs		X	X	R generally
GCMs			X	N/A
AODs			X	N/A
ISP papers			X	N/A

Document	Precedent	Evidence	Advice & Guidance	Retroactivity/ Prospectivity
CDOs			X	N/A
Announcements	(1)		X	N/A
Notices	(1)		X	N/A
New Releases			X	N/A
IRM			X	N/A
IRS Pubs.		X	X	R
Forms & Inst.			X	R
Handbooks............................		X	X	R usually
Oral Advice			X	N/A

(1) Announcements and Notices issued on or after December 28, 1987, and specifically designated as containing substantive or procedural guidance may be relied on to the same extent as revenue rulings and revenue procedures.

¶122 Appendix C—Effect of Revenue Rulings and Revenue Procedures on Previous Rulings

Revenue rulings and revenue procedures that have an effect on previous rulings use the following defined terms to describe the effect.

Amplified

The term "amplified" describes a situation where no change is being made in a prior published position, but the prior position is being extended to apply to a variation of the fact situation set forth therein. Thus, if an earlier ruling held that a principle applied to A, and the new ruling holds that the same principle also applies to B, the earlier ruling is amplified.

Clarified

The term "clarified" is used in those instances where the language in a prior ruling is being made clear because the language has caused, or may cause, some confusion. It is not used where a position in a prior ruling is being changed.

Distinguished

The term "distinguished" describes a situation where a ruling mentions a previously published ruling and points out an essential difference between them.

Modified

The term "modified" is used where the substance of a previously published position is being changed. Thus, if a prior ruling held that a principle applied to A but not to B, and the new ruling holds that it applies to both A and B, the prior ruling is modified because it corrects a published position.

Obsoleted

The term "obsoleted" describes a previously published ruling that is not considered determinative with respect to future transactions. Obsoleted is most commonly used in a ruling that lists previously published rulings that are obsoleted because of changes in law or regulations. A ruling may also be obsoleted because the substance has been included in regulations subsequently adopted.

Revoked

The term "revoked" describes situations where the position in the previously published ruling is not correct and the correct position is being stated in the new ruling.

Superseded

The term "superseded" describes a situation where the new ruling does nothing more than restate the substance and situation of a previously published ruling. Thus, superseded is used to republish under the 1986 Code and regulations the same position published under the 1954 Code and regulations. Superseded is also used when it is desired to republish in a single ruling a series of situations, names, and so forth, that were previously published over a period of time in separate rulings. If the new ruling does more than restate the substance of a prior ruling, a combination of terms is used. For example, *modified and superseded* describes a situation where the substance of a previously published ruling is being changed in part and is continued without change in part and it is desired to restate the valid portion of the previously published ruling in a new ruling that is self-contained. In this case the previously published ruling is first modified and then, as modified, is superseded.

Supplemented

The term "supplemented" is used in situations in which a list, such as a list of the names of countries, is published in a ruling and that list is expanded by adding further names in subsequent rulings. After the original ruling has been supplemented several times, a new ruling may be published that includes the list in the original ruling and the additions and that supersedes all prior rulings in the series.

Suspended

The term "suspended" is used in rare situations to show that the previous published rulings will not be applied pending some future action, such as the issuance of new or amended regulations, the outcome of cases in litigation, or the outcome of an IRS study.

¶123 Appendix D—Commonly Used Abbreviations for Tax Research Documents and References

The following is an alphabetical listing of commonly used abbreviations in tax research documents and resource materials. Many of the documents and resource materials mentioned here are for reference only and were not discussed in the text.

ACE	Adjusted current earnings
ACI	Appeals coordinated issue
Acq.	Acquiescence by IRS
ACRS	Accelerated cost recovery system
ACS	IRS automated collection system sites
ADP	IRS program that processes tax returns and related documents
ADR	Asset depreciation range system
Aff'd, aff'g	Affirmed, affirming
AGI	Adjusted gross income
AGO	Attorney General Opinion
AIMS	Audit information management system
AMT	Alternative minimum tax
Ann.	Announcement
AOD	Action on Decision
APA	Administrative Procedure Act
ARF	IRS archive and retrieval system
A.R.M.	Appeals and Review Memorandum
ATAT	Abusive tax avoidance transaction
AUR	IRS Automated Underreporter System
BAM	Background Advice Memorandum
BC	U.S. Bankruptcy Court
BTA	Board of Tax Appeals
CA	U.S. Court of Appeals
CA DC	U.S. Court of Appeals for the District of Columbia
CA FC	U.S. Court of Appeals for the Federal Circuit
C.B.	Cumulative Bulletin
CBS	Collection, Bankruptcy and Summonses Bulletin
C.C.A.	Chief Counsel Advice
CCDM	Chief Counsel Directive Manual
CCH Dec.	Decision number assigned by CCH to Tax Court or Board of Tax Appeals decision
C.C.M.	Chief Counsel Memorandum
C.D.O.	Commissioner Delegation Order
CDP	Collection due process
Cert.	Certiorari, granted or denied by the U.S. Supreme Court
CERT	Corporate equity reduction transaction
CFR	U.S. Code of Federal Regulations
C.G.O.	Comptroller General's Opinion

CIDS	Consolidated inventory distribution system
C.I.R.	Commissioner of the Internal Revenue Service
Circ.	Treasury Department Circular
ClsCt	U.S. Claims Court
CNOL	Consolidated net operating loss
COBE	Continuity of business enterprise
COD	Cancellation of debt income
Conf. Rept.	Conference Report
C.S.T.	Capital Stock Tax Ruling
CtCls	U.S. Court of Claims
DA	Disclosure authorization
D.C., Int. Rev. Cir., Rev. Cir., A&C Coll.	Department Circular
Del. Order	Delegation Order
DISC	Domestic international sales corporation
DOI	Discharge of indebtedness income
EFTPS	Electronic Federal Tax Payment System
EGTRRA	The Economic Growth and Tax Relief Reconciliation Act of 2001 (P.L. 107-16)
EIC	Earned income credit
EMS	Electronic Management System
ERO	Electronic return originator
En banc	As a whole. indicates that the full court rather than a one- or three-judge panel has participated in the decision
E.O.	Executive Order
EPCRS	Employee plans compliance resolution system
ERISA	Employee Retirement Income Security Act of 1974
ERTA	The Economic Recovery Tax Act of 1981
ESA	Education savings account
ESBT	Electing small business trust
ESOP	Employee stock ownership plan
E.T.	Estate Tax Ruling
Exr., Exrx.	Executor, Executrix
F., F.2d, F.3d or F.Supp.	Federal Case Reporter
FedCl	U.S. Court of Federal Claims
FICA	Federal Insurance Contributions Act
FIFO	First-in, first-out
FOIA	Freedom of Information Act
FPAA	Final partnership administrative adjustment
FPHC	Foreign personal holding company
F.R.	Federal Register
FS	Fact sheet
F.S.A.	Field Service Advice
FSC	Foreign sales corporation
FUTA	Federal Unemployment Tax Act
G.A.O.	General Administrative Order
GAO	General Accounting Office
GATT	General Agreement on Tariffs and Trade
G.C.M.	General Counsel Memorandum

G.C.O.	General Counsel's Order
GSTT	Generation skipping transfer tax
H.R.	House of Representatives Bill
HSA	Health savings account
IDC	Intangbile drilling costs
IDR	Information document request
IRA	Individual retirement account
I.R.B.	Internal Revenue Bulletin
IR-Circ.	Internal Revenue Circular
IR-Mim.	Internal Revenue Mimeograph
IR-News Rel.	Internal Revenue News Release
IR-Pub.	IRS Publication
IRM	Internal Revenue Manual
IRM Supp.	Internal Revenue Manual Supplement
ISP	Industry Specialization Program
I.T.	Income Tax Unit Ruling
I.T. Info.	Income Tax Information Release
JCT	Joint Committee on Taxation
JGTRRA	Jobs and Growth Tax Relief Reconciliation Act of 2003
LIFO	Last-in, first-out
LITC	Low Income Taxpayer Clinic
LMSB	IRS Large and Mid-size Business Division
L.O.	Law Opinion
LTR	Letter Ruling
M&E	Meals and entertainment
MACRS	Modified accelerated cost recovery system
Memo.	Memorandum Opinion of the Tax Court
Mim.	Mimeographed letter of the IRS
Mod, mod'g	Modified, modifying
MOU	Memorandum of understanding
MSA	Medical savings account
MSSP	Market Segment Specialization Program
NAFTA	North American Free Trade Agreement Implementation Act
NFTL	Notice of federal tax lien
NMTC	New markets tax credit
NOL	Net operating loss
Nonacq.	Nonacquiescence by the IRS
NPC	Notional principal contract
OBRA '89	Omnibus Budget Reconciliation Act of 1989
OBRA '90	Omnibus Budget Reconciliation Act of 1990
OBRA '93	Omnibus Budget Reconciliation Act of 1993
O.D.	Office Decision
OIC	Offer-in-compromise
OID	Original issue discount
Op. A.G.	Attorney General's Opinion
PAL	Passive activity loss

Per curiam	A judicial opinion of the whole court
PFA	Pre-filing agreement
PFIC	Passive foreign investment company
PHC	Personal holding company
PIA	Privacy impact assessment
P.L.	Public Law
PLR	Private Letter Ruling
PRP	IRS problem resolution program
PS	Pension Trust Service
Pub.	Publication (IRS Publication)
QDRO	Qualified domestic relations order
QEAA	Qualified exchange accomodation arrangement
QI	Qualified intermediary
QTIP	Qualified terminable interest property
RAL	Refund anticipation loan
Reg.	Qualified intermediary
Reh'g	Rehearing
REIT	Real estate investment trust
Rem'd, rem'g	Remanded, remanding
REMIC	Real estate mortgage investment conduit
Rev. Proc.	Revenue Procedure
Rev. Rul.	Revenue Ruling
Rev'd, rev'g	Reversed, reversing
REVRA '89	Revenue Reconciliation Act of 1989
REVRA '90	Revenue Reconciliation Act of 1990
REVRA '93	Revenue Reconciliation Act of 1993
R.S. (Rev. Stat.)	U.S. Revised Statutes
RIC	Regulated investment company
S.	Senate Bill
SAM	Strategic Advice Memorandum
S.M.	Solicitor's Memorandum
S.P.R.	Statement of Procedural Rules
S.S.T.	Social Security Tax Ruling
S.T.	Sales Tax Ruling
SB/SE	IRS Small Business/Self-Employed Division
SCt	U.S. Supreme Court Reporter
SEP	Simplified employee pension
SFR	Substitute for return
SIMPLE	Savings incentive match plan for employees
SOI	Statistics of income
Sol. Op.	Solicitor's Opinion
Sp. Rul.	Special Ruling
SPR	Statement of Procedural Rules
SRLY	Separate return limitation year
SSA	Social Security Administration
Sup.Ct.	U.S. Supreme Court Reporter
TAM	Technical Advice Memorandum
TAMRA	Technical and Miscellaneous Revenue Act of 1988

TAO	Taxpayer Assistance Order
TAS	Taxpayer Advocate Service
T.B.M.	Tax Board Memorandum
T.B.R.	Tax Board Recommendation
TBOR	Taxpayer Bill of Rights
TBOR2	Taxpayer Bill of Rights 2
TC	Tax Court Regular Decision
TCM	Tax Court Memorandum Decision
TCMP	Taxpayer Compliance Measurement Program
TCO	Taxpayer Compliance Officer
T.D.	Treasury Decision
TDA	Taxpayer delinquency account
T.D. News Rel.	Treasury Department News Release
T.D.O.	Treasury Department Order
TEAM	Technical Expedited Advice Memorandum
TEFRA	The Tax Equity and Fiscal Responsibility Act of 1982
TE/GE	IRS Tax Exempt and Government Entities Division
TFRP	Trust fund recovery penalty
TIA	Tax information authorization
TIGTA	Treasury Inspector General for Tax Administration
TIN	Taxpayer identification number
TIR	Technical Information Release
TLCATS	Tax Litigation Accounting and Control System
TM	Technical Memorandum
TMP	Tax matters partner
TRA '86	Tax Reform Act of 1986
TRA '97	Taxpayer Relief Act of 1997
UBIT	Unrelated business income tax
U.S.	Official U.S. Supreme Court Reporter
U.S.C.	United States Code
USTC	UNITED STATES TAX CASES (published by CCH, Incorporated)
VEBA	Voluntary Employees' Beneficiary Association
W&I	IRS Wage & Investment Operating Division

¶124 Appendix E—CCH Incorporated Partial Listing of Publications Reproducing and Explaining IRS Documents

The following is a partial listing of the CCH Incorporated publications that reproduce, summarize, and explain Internal Revenue Documents.

Standard Federal Tax Reports

The 25 volume CCH STANDARD FEDERAL TAX REPORTS contains authoritative sources of income tax law, arranged for quick and easy reference. Official contents include: Internal Revenue Code, with changes and amendments to date; official Income Tax Regulations interpreting the Code, with current amendments; Tax Court and Board of Tax Appeal cases; revenue rulings, revenue procedures, and other income tax items published in the Treasury Department's Internal Revenue Bulletin; and press releases and other IRS and Treasury Department issues. Throughout this reporter, CCH editorial features are combined with the official contents to assist in the solution of income tax problems.

CCH Federal Tax Service

The CCH FEDERAL TAX SERVICE is a comprehensive federal tax reference service providing complete coverage of the law of federal income, estate and gift taxation. The analysis is aimed at tax specialists and general practitioners. It is written by more than 250 leading tax practitioners who provide a practical, real-world focus. Includes practical examples, sample calculations, comments and planning notes that show how to apply tax principles.

CCH Guide to Car, Travel & Entertainment and Home Office Deductions

This publication walks the user through the ins and outs of claiming maximum deductions for common business expenses.

CCH Guide to Record Retention Requirements

The Guide is a single-source reference designed to keep individuals and businesses apprised of federal recordkeeping provisions as prescribed by the various agencies in the Code of Federal Regulations.

CYBERTAXATION: The Taxation of E-Commerce

This is a comprehensive and practical guide to help understand the important and rapidly evolving dynamics of electronic commerce.

Exempt Organizations Reports

The federal controls on the activities of tax-exempt organizations and private foundations are the subject of the CCH EXEMPT ORGANIZATIONS REPORTS. Also detailed are the state law requirements for exempt organizations, including the full texts of state statutes, tax laws, registration and reporting requirements, and any limitations on charitable contributions.

¶124

Family Tax Law Guide

The CCH FAMILY LAW TAX GUIDE provides full and continuing coverage of the federal tax aspects of family law—both as they relate to the family united and as they relate to the family in the process of divorce or separation.

Federal Estate and Gift Tax Reports

The three volume CCH FEDERAL ESTATE AND GIFT TAX REPORTS sets out the rules and regulations regarding estate, gift, and generation-skipping transfer taxes. Explanations, annotated with and based on authorities, clearly show what the rules mean and how to use them.

Federal Excise Tax Reports

This reference offers complete, timely coverage of federal excise taxes, with monthly reports of the latest developments and tax law changes.

Federal Income Taxes of Decedents, Estates and Trusts

CCH's FEDERAL INCOME TAXES OF DECEDENTS, ESTATES AND TRUSTS provides indepth coverage of the fundamental rules for preparing a decedent's final income tax return and highlights the income tax rules for the decedent's estate and related trusts.

Federal Tax Course

A one-of-a-kind resource for reference and training in tax—covering the vast realm of federal taxation with utmost clarity and painstaking attention to detail.

Federal Tax Forms

Reproduction-quality rendering of virtually all federal income, estate and gift tax forms, schedules and official instructions, plus those for employment, and private foundations, is provided.

Federal Tax Guide

The CCH FEDERAL TAX GUIDE provides a concise source that explains federal income, estate and gift, payroll and selected excise taxes.

Federal Tax Manual

This quick-reference manual offers line-by-line instruction on the preparation of tax returns as well as discussions on tax compliance. The manual reproduces major federal income tax return forms filled-in to demonstrate how specific rules apply.

Federal Taxation Practice and Procedure

Provides a clear explanation of the organization, structure and processes involved in IRS practice. A favorite in practice and procedure classes because of its clear descriptions and logical presentation, it is a top reference for practitioners as well. The book patiently covers the basics, the complexities and the details with plenty of real-life illustrations and examples. All the latest IRS structural changes and developments are explained, and the book helpfully includes reproductions of official letters, forms and notices used by the IRS.

Fiduciary Tax Guide

This handy practitioner's reference offers expert analysis of fiduciary tax issues that can help estate and trust administrators avoid turning personal responsibility into personal liability.

Financial and Estate Planning

CCH FINANCIAL AND ESTATE PLANNING is a total financial and estate planning reporter organized for professional use. It covers all stages of the estate plan, from development to administration.

Fringe Benefits Tax Guide

The CCH FRINGE BENEFITS TAX GUIDE provides quick, concise, and thorough answers to questions concerning the income and payroll tax treatment of "perks" from both the employer and employee standpoint.

Information Returns Guide

The CCH INFORMATION RETURNS GUIDE covers the federal information reporting rules for nonwage income, including interest, dividends and original issue discount, pensions and IRAs, payments received by brokers, and miscellaneous income. The Guide also contains the backup withholding rules that apply to the area of information reporting.

Internal Revenue Manual

The CCH INTERNAL REVENUE MANUAL reports key elements of the operating procedures of the IRS, with emphasis on such areas as audit and investigation, delinquent accounts, returns, and rulings.

IRS Letter Rulings Reports

CCH IRS LETTER RULINGS REPORTS features the full text of IRS responses to inquiries concerning application of the tax rules to specific situations along with the text of revenue procedures relating to the IRS Letter Rulings.

IRS Positions Reports

The full texts of official IRS documents, including General Counsel's Memoranda (GCMs), Technical Memoranda (TMs), Actions on Decisions (AODs), Market Segment Specialization Program (MSSP) audit guides, and Industry Specialization Program Papers (ISP papers), which form the "working law" of the agency and reflect final statements of IRS policy are reproduced in CCH IRS POSITIONS REPORTS.

IRS Publications

Full-text reproductions of tax publications issued by the federal government and intended for the use of taxpayers and their advisers are provided.

IRS Tax Collection Procedures

IRS TAX COLLECTION PROCEDURES presents valuable insights and practical, hands-on guidance in one comprehensive volume for all practitioners who represent clients before the Collections Division of the IRS.

Limited Liability Company Guide

This practice-oriented guide offers guidance on federal income tax planning and compliance issues and covers state tax and business law requirements. Explanations cover the formation, operation, and dissolution of an LLC. Full-text federal cases and rulings demonstrate how LLC law is evolving.

Partnership Tax Planning and Practice

This guide includes explanations, tax planning, choice of entity considerations, sample agreements and compliance forms. Includes a monthly newsletter that provides news of the latest cases, rulings, and other developments impacting partnerships.

Payroll Management Guide

The guidance needed for managing payroll operations and complying with changing federal, state, and local rules is provided. Federal and state income, social security and medicare tax deductions, employers' taxes, and wages and hours information are also included.

Pension Plan Guide

Income tax angles, as well as other tax, legal, and practical developments affecting pension and profit-sharing plans and employee benefits are explored in CCH PENSION PLAN GUIDE.

Retirement Benefits Tax Guide

The RETIREMENT BENEFITS TAX GUIDE is designed as a comprehensive source of information on the federal taxation of retirement benefits.

S Corporations Guide

The S CORPORATION GUIDE supplies comprehensive analysis of the tax laws that apply to S Corporations and their shareholders. Also includes a monthly report letter that provides news on the latest developments for S corporations and their shareholders.

Tax Court Reports

The full texts of regular and memo decisions of the U.S. Tax Court are published currently in CCH TAX COURT REPORTS. D ecisions on income, estate, and gift tax issues are reported, with timely information on pending petitions and an Index-Digest to decided issues.

U.S. Master Tax Guide

CCH's U.S. MASTER TAX GUIDE is the number one tax handbook available for tax professionals. It reflects all pertinent federal tax law changes, to date of

¶124

publication, that affect filing current returns and provides fast and reliable answers to tax questions affecting individuals and business income tax.

U.S. Master Compensation Tax Guide

CCH's U.S. MASTER COMPENSATION TAX GUIDE offers concise, practical coverage of the federal tax laws concerning executive and employee compensation. This guide covers all of the common forms of compensation, including: salary, bonuses and other current compensation, employee fringe benefits, qualified deferred compensation, and nonqualified deferred compensation.

U.S. Master Depreciation Guide

CCH's U.S. MASTER DEPRECIATION GUIDE offers tax and accounting professionals who work with businesses a one-stop resource for guidance in understanding and applying the complex depreciation rules.

U.S. Master Excise Tax Guide

CCH's U.S. MASTER EXCISE TAX GUIDE provides a thorough explanation of all federal excise taxes.

Journal of Passthrough Entities

The CCH JOURNAL OF PASSTHROUGH ENTITIES focuses on issues affecting all forms of passthrough entities: partnerships, S corporations and LLCs. It offers comprehensive, indepth articles on subjects of interest with an answer-oriented, practical-application slant, providing valuable advice on tested strategies, telling you what works, what doesn't work, and why.

Journal of Tax Practice and Procedure

The JOURNAL OF TAX PRACTICE AND PROCEDURE is devoted entirely to the complex area of representing taxpayers before the IRS, from initial contact through litigation. The journal emphasizes taxpayer advocacy and the protection of taxpayer and representative rights, analyzes legislative and regulatory changes, and highlights industry shifts that present taxpayer representation issues.

Journal of Taxation of Financial Products

The JOURNAL OF TAXATION OF FINANCIAL PRODUCTS emphasizes the tax treatment of hedges, identifying strategies to maximize the tax-inclusive return for investment vehicles and cross-border derivative transactions, and examining the tax uncertainty from new derivative products. It includes comprehensive, indepth articles, along with valuable advice and proven strategies from practicing professionals, plus "head's Up" notice of financial products taxation policies and trends, and helpful planning tips.

¶124

Index

References are to paragraph (¶) numbers.

STO